Vocabulary Power

Teacher's Guide
Grade 4

Copyright © by Harcourt, Inc.

All rights reserved. No part of this publication may be reproduced or transmitted in any form or by any means, electronic or mechanical, including photocopy, recording, or any information storage and retrieval system, without permission in writing from the publisher.

Permission is hereby granted to individual teachers using the corresponding student's textbook or kit as the major vehicle for regular classroom instruction to photocopy complete student pages from this publication in classroom quantities for instructional use and not for resale.

Duplication of this work other than by individual classroom teachers under the conditions specified above requires a license. To order a license to duplicate this work in greater than classroom quantities, contact Customer Service, Harcourt, Inc., 6277 Sea Harbor Drive, Orlando, Florida 32887-6777. Telephone: 1-800-225-5425. Fax: 1-800-874-6418 or 407-352-3445.

HARCOURT and the Harcourt Logo are trademarks of Harcourt, Inc.

Printed in the United States of America

ISBN 0-15-320248-3

6 7 8 9 10 11 12   082   2007 2006 2005 2004

Table of Contents

Introduction T3

How to Use This Book T4

Informal Assessment Ideas T5

Weekly Instructional Plans T6

Resources for Teachers

    Activities T12

    Graphic Organizers T18

    Word Lists T20

Word Cards T25

Vocabulary Power Student Book i

Copying Masters 1

Glossary 109

My Own Word List 123

Introduction

Research Findings

Research documents the relationship between vocabulary knowledge, reading comprehension, and oral and written expression. The more words students acquire, the better chance they will have for success in reading, writing, and spelling. **Vocabulary Power** is a **vocabulary development program** that will promote students' "word consciousness"—their awareness of and interest in words.

From research we know that children learn between 1,000 and 5,000 words per year—and the average child learns about 3,000 words. We also know that wide reading is the most effective technique for increasing vocabulary. However, practice has demonstrated that 300–500 words per year can be taught through direct instruction.

A vocabulary program must help students experience words by

- **hearing** and **seeing** words used;
- **discussing** and **defining** meanings of words;
- **reading** and **writing** words in meaningful contexts.

In addition to helping students broaden and expand their vocabularies, a vocabulary program must also help them learn techniques for independent vocabulary acquisition.

Fostering Vocabulary Development

In **Vocabulary Power** students learn through daily activities that actively involve them in listening, speaking, reading, and writing. These activities

- **present** them with words from their own oral vocabularies, words that they also need to decode and to read;
- **introduce** them to new concepts and words, and to new labels for familiar concepts;
- **show** them how words are properly used and how our language works;
- **provide** opportunities for discussions, an important dimension of vocabulary development.

The activities in **Vocabulary Power** encourage comprehension and associative thinking. Students learn both the definitions of the vocabulary words and how the words function in different contexts. Their tasks may include

- ☑ to identify or supply synonyms, antonyms, or related words;
- ☑ to generate lists of new or known words;
- ☑ to classify, categorize, compare, contrast, illustrate;
- ☑ to create original sentences.

Many tasks are open-ended to encourage discussion and sharing of ideas.

How to Use This Book

Overview

The **instructional plan** for the *Vocabulary Power Teacher's Guide* introduces eight vocabulary words per week for 36 weeks. You can find the lists of these vocabulary words in the Weekly Instructional Plans section of this guide on pages T6–T11. Some words in these lists appear in boldface type. These are designated as Power Words because they provide the springboard for learning the rest of the Words of the Week and for relating the Words of the Week to each other.

The *Vocabulary Power Teacher's Guide* also includes

- ideas for informal assessment;
- activities and word lists to engage learners;
- 288 reproducible Word Cards to be reproduced and cut apart for use in whole class or in small group instruction.

See pages T12–T24 for additional ideas and suggestions.

Weekly Plan

Each weekly plan provides five days of vocabulary assignments. As you work through these assignments, you can contribute to students' success by

- using the words throughout the day as part of your own vocabulary;
- having students look for the words in newspapers and magazines;
- using the words in classroom contests or as part of classroom business;
- maintaining a chart of "Word Sightings" in the classroom;
- keeping dictionaries on hand and encouraging students to use them;
- encouraging students to keep their own word lists and to use words from these lists in their daily writing.

The Weekly Instructional Plans on pages T6–T11 of this guide contain specific plans based upon the following model:

DAY 1	Introduce and discuss the Power Word.
DAY 2	Introduce the remaining seven Words of the Week. Complete the first worksheet.
DAY 3	Review words. Complete the second worksheet.
DAY 4	Review words. Complete the third worksheet.
DAY 5	Review words. Do an assessment activity.

Informal Assessment Ideas

WEEKLY

Have students demonstrate knowledge using one or more of the following techniques.

Kid Watching

Observe students daily in informal situations.

- Do you hear them use the words in playground talk, in conversations, or in classroom discussions?
- Do they attempt to use the words in their own writing?
- Do they mention seeing or hearing the words on television or radio, or seeing the words in printed materials?

Self-Assessment/Peer Assessment

As words are introduced each week, have students create a Rating Chart with the following headings: *Know this word / Have seen or heard this word / Don't know this word.* Have them return to this chart periodically to make adjustments or to update their responses. Suggest that students determine if they need to spend more time with any of the words.

Have students maintain a log of *when*, *where*, or *how* they saw or heard any of the Words of the Week, or maintain a chart in the classroom where you can record "Word Sightings."

Assessment Activities

Plan activities to have students demonstrate their knowledge and understanding of the Words of the Week. The activities may or may not be timed. You might have students match each word with its definition or have them define a word in one of these ways:

- ✔ use the word in a sentence
- ✔ write another word that has a similar meaning
- ✔ write a word that has a meaning opposite to the word
- ✔ indicate its semantic features (prefix, suffix, compound word, and so on)
- ✔ provide an example (written or drawn)
- ✔ provide a statement of how the example compares/contrasts to another word
- ✔ show the relationship of a part to the whole or vice versa
- ✔ present the word in a graphic manner that shows its meaning

END OF UNIT

Have students demonstrate knowledge through one of the following techniques:

Conduct an Open Sort

Select a representative group of words and have students organize the words into categories of their own choosing.

Conduct a Closed Sort

Distribute to students a representative group of words and a list of categories. Have them categorize the words appropriately.

Weekly Instructional Plans

Chapter 1	**WORDS OF THE WEEK:** employment, livelihood, **occupation**, position, profession, pursuit, specialization, vocation
DAY 1	USAGE Introduce and define *occupation*. **Teaching is my occupation. What are some other occupations?**
DAY 2 p. 1	CONNOTATION/DENOTATION **What are some synonyms for *occupation*?** Discuss how the synonyms differ from each other.
DAY 3 p. 2	SUFFIXES Write *occupation* on the board. **What is the base word? What is the suffix?** (See also *Vocabulary Power*, page 2.)
DAY 4 p. 3	ANALOGIES; COMPARE/CONTRAST **How would you complete this analogy: "Waitress is to occupation as Thanksgiving is to ___."** Discuss responses.
DAY 5	USAGE Ask students to choose a category, such as "animals" or "books," and to write a list of occupations related to that category.

Chapter 2	**WORDS OF THE WEEK:** auctioneer, engineer, jeweler, mountaineer, photographer, pioneer, senator, **volunteer**
DAY 1	USAGE Introduce and define *volunteer*. **What could a volunteer do?**
DAY 2 p. 4	SUFFIXES **What does a painter do? What do you call someone who dances?**
DAY 3 p. 5	MULTIPLE-MEANING WORDS Ask students to use *volunteer* first as a noun in a sentence, then as a verb in a sentence.
DAY 4 p. 6	DICTIONARY Remind students of the purpose of guide words in a dictionary. **The guide words on a dictionary page are *village* and *volume*. Would *volunteer* appear on this page?**
DAY 5	EXEMPLIFICATION **Make a list of good things about being a volunteer.**

Chapter 3	**WORDS OF THE WEEK:** approximately, barely, exactly, inaccurately, nearly, precisely, roughly, virtually
DAY 1	SYNONYM Introduce and define *approximately*. **What is a synonym for *approximately*?**
DAY 2 p. 7	EXPLORE WORD MEANINGS **What is an antonym for *approximately*?**
DAY 3 p. 8	SUFFIXES Write *approximately* on the board. **What is the root word in *approximately*? What is the suffix? How does the suffix change the word's meaning?**
DAY 4 p. 9	GRADIENT ANALYSIS **If you needed a very good idea of how much something weighed, would you measure its weight roughly or precisely?**
DAY 5	APPLICATION Draw the picture that each of these sentences describes: "The dot is *exactly* on the line." "The dot is *approximately* on the line." Label the pictures.

Chapter 4	**WORDS OF THE WEEK:** budget, business, credit, currency, debt, **economy**, resources, spending
DAY 1	USAGE Introduce and define *economy*. Ask students to discuss how earning and spending money affects the economy.
DAY 2 p. 10	CLASSIFY/CATEGORIZE Write on the board: *nickels, pennies, checks, dimes*. **Which word does not belong in this group? What category do the other words fit into?**
DAY 3 p. 11	CONTEXT CLUES Have students use context clues to determine the meaning of *debt* in this sentence: **Peter has borrowed a lot of money and is in debt.**
DAY 4 p. 12	COMPARE/CONTRAST **Having a credit card is like having money except ___.**
DAY 5	EXEMPLIFICATION **How are banks a part of our economy?**

Chapter 5	**WORDS OF THE WEEK:** arts, civilization, cuisine, **culture**, ethnicity, folklore, language, society
DAY 1	CLASSIFICATION Introduce and define *culture*. **Language is a part of a group's culture. What is another part of a group's culture?**
DAY 2 p. 13	CONTENT-AREA WORDS **Culture has one meaning in science and a different meaning in social studies. What is the social studies meaning?**
DAY 3 p. 14	WORD FAMILIES Write *culture, cultural,* and *cultured* on the board. **What base word do these words have in common?**
DAY 4 p. 15	RELATED WORDS Write *cuisine, chili,* and *classroom*. **Which two words are related?**
DAY 5	EXEMPLIFICATION **Can you name an example of a culture?** Discuss the customs of various cultures.

Chapter 6	**WORDS OF THE WEEK:** autobiography, autograph, **biography**, diary, interview, journal, memoir, photograph
DAY 1	EXEMPLIFICATION Introduce and define *biography*. **What could be the title of a biography?**
DAY 2 p. 16	CLASSIFY/CATEGORIZE **What label describes books, magazines, and newspapers?**
DAY 3 p. 17	GREEK ROOTS Write *biography* and *autograph*. **What do these words have in common? What is the meaning of *bio-*?**
DAY 4 p. 18	COMPARE/CONTRAST Write *biography* and *autobiography* on the board. **How are these words alike? How are they different?**
DAY 5	GRAPHICS Design a book cover for a biography of a person you admire. Come up with a title for the book.

T6 Vocabulary Power Teacher's Guide

Chapter 7	**WORDS OF THE WEEK:** anatomy, composition, form, frame, framework, mold, skeleton, structure
DAY 1	USAGE Introduce and define *anatomy*. Ask students: Who would need to study human anatomy?
DAY 2 p. 19	MULTIPLE-MEANING WORDS An object has a *form* or shape. What other meaning can *form* have?
DAY 3 p. 20	CONTENT-AREA WORDS What major parts of the human body might you learn about in an anatomy class? What words might you use in a cooking class?
DAY 4 p. 21	SYNONYMS Point out that while *anatomy* refers to the study of the body, it also means the actual form of the body. What other words have the same meaning as *form*?
DAY 5	EXEMPLIFICATION Anatomy is the science or study of the human form. Write a list of other fields of study.

Chapter 8	**WORDS OF THE WEEK:** alpine, aquatic, arctic, arid, habitat, subterranean, temperate, tropical
DAY 1	SYNONYMS Introduce and define *habitat*. What is a synonym for *habitat*?
DAY 2 p. 22	CLASSIFY/CATEGORIZE What animals live in an aquatic habitat?
DAY 3 p. 23	ANALOGIES Complete this analogy by naming the appropriate habitat: Ocean is to whales as _____ is to camels.
DAY 4 p. 24	WORD FAMILIES Habitats, inhabited, inhabitants. What is the root or base word of this family?
DAY 5	EXEMPLIFICATION Work in pairs. Write a list of animals and their appropriate habitats.

Chapter 9	**WORDS OF THE WEEK:** arrangement, continuous, order, organization, progression, sequel, sequence, subsequent
DAY 1	USAGE Introduce and define *sequence*. Why is *sequence* important when you follow directions?
DAY 2 p. 25	CONTEXT CLUES When would you use the word *sequence* instead of *arrangement*?
DAY 3 p. 26	EXPLORE WORD MEANING How many ways can you use the word *arrangement*?
DAY 4 p. 27	SYNONYMS What is a synonym for *sequence*?
DAY 5	EXEMPLIFICATION On a sheet of paper, write the sequence of events in your favorite book or movie.

Chapter 10	**WORDS OF THE WEEK:** geographer, geologist, gravity, magma, petroleum, sediment, seismograph, volcanic
DAY 1	USAGE Introduce and define *geologist*. What do geologists study?
DAY 2 p. 28	CLASSIFY/CATEGORIZE Write *geologist, biologist, chemist,* and *astronomer* on the board. Name a category that all four of these words fit into.
DAY 3 p. 29	COMPARE/CONTRAST How are snow and rain alike? How are they different?
DAY 4 p. 30	SUFFIXES Write *geologist, economist,* and *novelist* on the board. What is the suffix in each of these words? What does it mean?
DAY 5	SYNONYMS Is *scientist* a good synonym for *geologist*?

Chapter 11	**WORDS OF THE WEEK:** coastal, marine, mariner, maritime, nautical, naval, oceanic, submarine
DAY 1	CLASSIFICATION Introduce and define *marine*. What animals or plants live in a marine environment?
DAY 2 p. 31	EXPLORE WORD MEANING Write *marine, mariner*. What is a mariner? What clues helped you figure out the word?
DAY 3 p. 32	ANALOGIES Complete this analogy: marine is to fish as land is to _____.
DAY 4 p. 33	CONTENT-AREA WORDS Write *oceans* on the board. What are some categories that could be added to a web about oceans?
DAY 5	EXEMPLIFICATION Write a job description for a *marine photographer*. List the equipment he or she might use. Repeat for a *marine geologist*.

Chapter 12	**WORDS OF THE WEEK:** blossom, flourish, flower, progress, prosper, succeed, survive, thrive
DAY 1	EXEMPLIFICATION Introduce and define *thrive*. What might help a plant thrive?
DAY 2 p. 34	EXPLORE WORD MEANINGS Describe what is happening if a business is thriving.
DAY 3 p. 35	HOMOPHONES AND HOMOGRAPHS Write *hare* and *hair*. What do these words mean? Write *wind*. How can this word be pronounced? What meanings does it have?
DAY 4 p. 36	CONNOTATION/DENOTATION *Thrive* and *grow* are synonyms. Which has a more positive connotation?
DAY 5	Would you rather thrive or prosper? Why?

Weekly Instructional Plans

Chapter 13	WORDS OF THE WEEK: acrylic, bristle, **canvas**, easel, impression, landscape, palette, subject
DAY 1	USAGE Introduce and define *canvas*. What is canvas used for?
DAY 2 p. 37	CONTENT-AREA WORDS Name some words that are related to art.
DAY 3 p. 38	MULTIPLE-MEANING WORDS In what ways can you use the word *paint*?
DAY 4 p. 39	ANALOGIES Complete this analogy: Canvas is to artist as _____ is to musician.
DAY 5	EXEMPLIFICATION Make a list of materials artists use to paint or draw.

Chapter 14	WORDS OF THE WEEK: fable, fiction, folktale, **literature**, myth, narrative, nonfiction, poetry
DAY 1	USAGE Introduce and define *literature*. Name some types of literature.
DAY 2 p. 40	EXPLORE WORD MEANING Write *literature, folktales, nonfiction*. What one word in this group describes the others?
DAY 3 p. 41	ANALOGIES A peach is a kind of fruit. What is a kind of literature?
DAY 4 p. 42	ANTONYMS *Fiction* and *nonfiction* have opposite meanings. What are some other antonyms?
DAY 5	EXEMPLIFICATION Make a list of your favorite books or authors.

Chapter 15	WORDS OF THE WEEK: chance, circumstance, happenstance, occasion, occurrence, **opportunity**, probability, serendipity
DAY 1	USAGE Introduce and define *opportunity*. You have a chance to go skiing. What weather conditions will make this a positive opportunity?
DAY 2 p. 43	SYNONYMS What is a synonym for *opportunity*?
DAY 3 p. 44	CLASSIFY/CATEGORIZE Write *serendipity, fortune,* and *happenstance* on the board. What do these words have in common?
DAY 4 p. 45	WORDS IN CONTEXT; DICTIONARY When might you use the phrase "there's a chance of"?
DAY 5	COMPARISON Complete this statement: *Serendipity* is like *opportunity* because _____.

Chapter 16	WORDS OF THE WEEK: **choreograph**, choreographer, compose, conduct, conductor, entertain, orchestrate, perform
DAY 1	COMPARISON Introduce and define *choreograph*. How is choreographing a dance like putting together a puzzle?
DAY 2 p. 46	CLASSIFY/CATEGORIZE Name a category that includes: choreographer, conductor, composer.
DAY 3 p. 47	SUFFIXES Write on the board: *choreograph, conduct*. Add an ending to each word to make it mean "one who."
DAY 4 p. 48	COMPARE/CONTRAST How are *choreograph* and *dance* alike? How are they different?
DAY 5	COMPARE/CONTRAST Complete these statements: A choreographer is like a composer except _____. A choreographer is like a conductor except _____.

Chapter 17	WORDS OF THE WEEK: carnival, **carousel**, gilded, melodious, musical, ornate, rotating, whirligig
DAY 1	CLASSIFICATION Introduce and define *carousel*. Where might you see a carousel?
DAY 2 p. 49	RELATED WORDS What words could describe a carousel?
DAY 3 p. 50	CONTEXT CLUES Write on the board: *I don't like the rotating rides, because spinning around makes me dizzy.* What words help you figure out what *rotating* means?
DAY 4 p. 51	COMPARE/CONTRAST Name a difference between a pony ride and a carousel ride. Now name a similarity.
DAY 5	DESCRIPTIVE LANGUAGE Write a paragraph describing a carousel, from either a spectator's or rider's perspective.

Chapter 18	WORDS OF THE WEEK: dedication, monument, **pedestal**, pedestrian, plaque, podiatrist, scaffold, sculpt
DAY 1	EXEMPLIFICATION Introduce and define *pedestal*. What might you place on a pedestal?
DAY 2 p. 52	RELATED WORDS How are *pedestal* and *monument* related? How are *pedestal* and *pedestrian* related?
DAY 3 p. 53	GREEK AND LATIN ROOTS The root *ped-* comes from the Latin for *foot*. Name some other words with this root.
DAY 4 p. 54	EXPLORE WORD MEANING What is the purpose of a dedication?
DAY 5	FIGURATIVE LANGUAGE What does the phrase "put someone on a pedestal" mean? How is being "put on a pedestal" like being a statue?

Chapter 19	WORDS OF THE WEEK: ambiance, **atmosphere**, climate, oxygen, ozone, smog, surrounding, vapor
DAY 1	USAGE Introduce and define *atmosphere*. **Why do we need a clean atmosphere?**
DAY 2 p. 55	EXPLORE WORD MEANING **How are *atmosphere* and *oxygen* related?**
DAY 3 p. 56	MULTIPLE-MEANING WORDS **What does *atmosphere* mean in the sentence Their house has a pleasant atmosphere?**
DAY 4 p. 57	CLASSIFY/CATEGORIZE Write *atmosphere*, *ozone*, and *oxygen*. **How are these words related?**
DAY 5	COMPARE/CONTRAST **What is more important for a restaurant to have, a good atmosphere or good food?**

Chapter 22	WORDS OF THE WEEK: arboretum, botanical, **botanist**, botany, flora, foliage, greenhouse, vegetation
DAY 1	EXPLORE WORD MEANING Introduce and define *botanist*. **Would a botanist be more likely to work at a garden or a zoo? Why?**
DAY 2 p. 64	CONTEXT CLUES **What words in this sentence help you figure out the meaning of the word cycle: A botanist must carefully study a plant's growth in order to record its life cycle.**
DAY 3 p. 65	CLASSIFY/CATEGORIZE Write *botanist*, *geologist*, and *astronomer* on the board. **What do all three of these words have in common?**
DAY 4 p. 66	COMPARE/CONTRAST **How is *botany* like *biology*? How is it different?**
DAY 5	EXEMPLIFICATION **Make a list of the kinds of trees and flowers a botanist might study if he or she came to your community.**

Chapter 20	WORDS OF THE WEEK: aster, asterisk, asteroid, astral, astrodome, astronaut, astronautics, **astronomer**
DAY 1	USAGE Introduce and define *astronomer*. **Could there be astronauts if we didn't have astronomers?**
DAY 2 p. 58	GREEK AND LATIN ROOTS *Astro* is a root meaning star. **What does astronomy mean?**
DAY 3 p. 59	COMPARE/CONTRAST **Complete the statement: An astronomer is like an astronaut but _____.**
DAY 4 p. 60	RELATED WORDS Write *telescope* and *microscope* on the board. **How are these words related?**
DAY 5	CONTENT-AREA WORDS **List some words that an astronomer might use.**

Chapter 23	WORDS OF THE WEEK: abrasion, coastline, **erosion**, glacier, gravel, wear, weathering, windswept
DAY 1	EXEMPLIFICATION Introduce and define *erosion*. Ask students: **What are some forces that cause erosion?**
DAY 2 p. 67	CONTENT AREA WORDS **In what subject could you expect to find words such as *erosion* and *weathering*? How are these words related?**
DAY 3 p. 68	ANALOGIES **In an analogy two pairs of words are related in the same way. Dunes are made of sand. Glaciers are made of _____.** Have students restate this in the form of an analogy.
DAY 4 p. 69	SYNONYMS AND ANTONYMS Write on the board The river flowed *swiftly*. **Provide a synonym for the underlined word. Provide an antonym.**
DAY 5	USAGE **Where might you find the effects of erosion?**

Chapter 21	WORDS OF THE WEEK: auditory, diurnal, **extra-sensitive**, extraordinary, nocturnal, ocular, olfactory, perception
DAY 1	CLASSIFY Introduce and define *extra-sensitive*. **Name an animal with extra-sensitive hearing and smell.**
DAY 2 p. 61	RELATED WORDS **How are *olfactory* and *auditory* related?**
DAY 3 p. 62	PREFIXES Write *extra-sensitive* on the board. **Does this word have a prefix? What is it and what does it mean?**
DAY 4 p. 63	ANALOGIES **Complete this analogy: Ears are to hearing as eyes are to _____.**
DAY 5	WORD FAMILIES **Extra-sensitive and senseless are in the same word family. Make a list of other words that would be in the same family as extra-sensitive.**

Chapter 24	WORDS OF THE WEEK: demolish, destroy, **devastate**, obliterate, refurbish, renovate, restore, revive
DAY 1	ANTONYMS Introduce and define *devastate*. Write the following and have students complete it. **Revive is/is not an antonym for devastate because _____.**
DAY 2 p. 70	SYNONYMS Write *hurt*, *destroy*, and *devastate* on the board. **Are these words synonyms? How are they alike? Different?**
DAY 3 p. 71	WORD FAMILIES **What are some words that are in the same family as *devastate*?**
DAY 4 p. 72	EXPLORE WORD MEANING **How can a hurricane devastate a coastal community?**
DAY 5	GRAPHICS **Write the word *devastate* in a manner that shows its meaning.**

Weekly Instructional Plans T9

Chapter 25	WORDS OF THE WEEK: boulevard, civic, downtown, metropolitan, municipal, skyscraper, subway, **urban**
DAY 1	ANTONYM Introduce and define *urban*. **What is an antonym for *urban*?**
DAY 2 p. 73	COMPARE/CONTRAST **How would life be similar in a large urban area and a small urban area? Different?**
DAY 3 p. 74	COMPOUND WORDS; COINED WORDS Write *down* and *town* on the board. Ask: **What compound word can you make with these words? What does it mean?**
DAY 4 p. 75	CONNOTATION/DENOTATION **Which sounds larger, a lane or a street? An alley or a sidestreet?**
DAY 5	ANALOGIES **Complete this analogy: Urban is to high-rise as _____ is to _____.**

Chapter 26	WORDS OF THE WEEK: ancestor, genealogy, heredity, **heritage**, history, inheritance, legacy, origin
DAY 1	CLASSIFICATION Introduce and define *heritage*. Traditions may be a part of someone's heritage. **What is another part of one's heritage?**
DAY 2 p. 76	EXPLORE WORD MEANING **If someone was interested in your family's origins, what kind of information would he or she be looking for?**
DAY 3 p. 77	CONTEXT CLUES **In the following sentence, what is the meaning of *origin*?** *The origin of this custom has been traced to Ghana.*
DAY 4 p. 78	CLASSIFY/CATEGORIZE **What are some customs a family might share that are part of its heritage?**
DAY 5	COMPARE/CONTRAST **How is *heritage* like an *inheritance*? How is it different?**

Chapter 27	WORDS OF THE WEEK: transatlantic, **transcontinental**, translate, translucent, transmountain, transoceanic, transparent, transport
DAY 1	SYNONYMS Introduce and define *transcontinental*. **What is a synonym for *transcontinental*?**
DAY 2 p. 79	CONTEXT CLUES **What context clues tell the meaning of *transcontinental* in this sentence?** *The transcontinental train traveled from the Pacific coast to the Atlantic coast.*
DAY 3 p. 80	EXPLORE WORD MEANING **Could *transcontinental* be the same as *across the country*?**
DAY 4 p. 81	WORD FAMILIES Write *transcontinental* and *continental* on the board. **How are these words related?**
DAY 5	USAGE **Could a river be transcontinental? Could a railroad? Make a list of things that could be described as transcontinental.**

Chapter 28	WORDS OF THE WEEK: aqueduct, canal, drench, hydrate, **irrigate**, moisten, sluice, trough
DAY 1	USAGE Introduce and define *irrigate*. **When would a farmer need to irrigate a field?**
DAY 2 p. 82	RELATED WORDS Words can be related by meaning or structural element. **How are *irrigate* and *moisten* related? What is another word with similar meaning?**
DAY 3 p. 83	WORD FAMILIES Write *irrigate* and *irrigation* on the board. **What root or base do these two words have in common?**
DAY 4 p. 84	CONTEXT CLUES **Listen to this sentence:** *In dry regions, farmers irrigate, or bring water to, their crops.* **What words give clues to the meaning of *irrigate*?**
DAY 5	COMPARISON Irrigating crops is like watering flowerbeds. **Think of another comparison.**

Chapter 29	WORDS OF THE WEEK: **delta**, inlet, meander, oasis, source, tidal, tributary, valley
DAY 1	USAGE Introduce and define *delta*. **Where would a delta form?**
DAY 2 p. 85	RELATED WORDS **If you had to write a paragraph about a river delta, what words or concepts could you use?**
DAY 3 p. 86	COMPARE/CONTRAST **How is a delta like a plain? Different?**
DAY 4 p. 87	ANALOGIES **Complete this analogy: Source is to delta as _____ is to end.**
DAY 5	GRAPHICS **Draw a diagram of a river, its mouth, and a delta. Label the parts.**

Chapter 30	WORDS OF THE WEEK: **amphibian**, amphibious, arachnid, crustacean, invertebrate, mammal, reptilian, vertebrate
DAY 1	EXEMPLIFICATION Introduce and define *amphibian*. **Why is a frog considered an amphibian?**
DAY 2 p. 88	CLASSIFY/CATEGORIZE Write *toad*, *mudskipper*, and *frog* on the board. **Name a category that would cover all three of these words.**
DAY 3 p. 89	WORD FAMILIES Write *amphibian* and *reptilian*. **What word part do these words have in common?**
DAY 4 p. 90	COMPARE/CONTRAST **How are amphibians and reptiles alike? Different?**
DAY 5	CLASSIFICATION Write *amphibian* and *mammal*. **Make lists of animals that fit these categories.**

Chapter 31	**WORDS OF THE WEEK:** amusement, diversion, leisure, pastime, pleasure, **recreation**, relaxation, repose
DAY 1	ANTONYM Introduce and define *recreation*. What is an antonym for *recreation*?
DAY 2 p. 91	RHYMING WORDS What word rhymes with *recreation* and means "a break from school or work"?
DAY 3 p. 92	CONNOTATION/DENOTATION Would you rather do something for *amusement* or *relaxation*? Why?
DAY 4 p. 93	SYNONYMS What is a synonym for *recreation*?
DAY 5	EXEMPLIFICATION List some popular forms of *recreation*.

Chapter 32	**WORDS OF THE WEEK:** **amateur**, beginner, dabbler, fledgling, novice, professional, rookie, trainee
DAY 1	USAGE Introduce and define *amateur*. Could an amateur win a competition? Get paid for his or her skill?
DAY 2 p. 94	COMPARE/CONTRAST An amateur is like a trainee except _____.
DAY 3 p. 95	EUPHEMISMS You may describe someone else as a *fledgling*, but you would rather be known as an _____. (*amateur*)
DAY 4 p. 96	ANTONYMS; COLLOQUIALISMS Name a word that means the opposite of *amateur*.
DAY 5	EXEMPLIFICATION Make a list of things you could participate in as an amateur.

Chapter 33	**WORDS OF THE WEEK:** colorful, descriptive, emphatic, picturesque, radiant, vibrant, vivacious, **vivid**
DAY 1	USAGE Introduce and define *vivid*. What could you describe as *vivid*?
DAY 2 p. 97	CLASSIFY/CATEGORIZE Write *vivid* and *emphatic* on the board. Which of these words could be used to describe language? A person? An image?
DAY 3 p. 98	WORDS IN CONTEXT Name a vivid color. A vivid word.
DAY 4 p. 99	WORD LINES Write *bright red*, *red*, and *fire-engine red* on the board. Arrange these words on a word line starting with the least vivid and ending with the most vivid.
DAY 5	EXEMPLIFICATION Make a list of vivid words an author might use to replace the verbs *say* and *walk*.

Chapter 34	**WORDS OF THE WEEK:** **competition**, conflict, contender, meet, opponent, rival, tournament, victor
DAY 1	EXEMPLIFICATION Introduce and define *competition*. What are some kinds of *competition*?
DAY 2 p. 100	ANALOGIES; RHYMING WORDS Complete this analogy: Competition is to contest as happy is to _____.
DAY 3 p. 101	WORD FAMILIES Write on the board *competition*, *competitor*, and *competitive*. What base word is common to these words?
DAY 4 p. 102	CLASSIFY/CATEGORIZE Write *players*, *contestants*, and *participants*. What category do these words belong to?
DAY 5	COMPARE/CONTRAST How is a competition like a test? Different?

Chapter 35	**WORDS OF THE WEEK:** deficient, essential, revitalize, supplement, vigor, vital, vitality, **vitamin**
DAY 1	RELATED WORDS Introduce and define *vitamin*. Vitamins are important to your health. What else is important?
DAY 2 p. 103	ANALOGIES Complete this analogy: Vitamins are to good health as _____ is to crops.
DAY 3 p. 104	LATIN ROOTS Write *vitamin* and *vital* on the board. What word part do these two words have in common?
DAY 4 p. 105	CONTEXT CLUES In the following sentence, what words are clues to the meaning of *vitamins*? *Foods rich in vitamins keep your body strong and healthy.*
DAY 5	USAGE Name some ways to add vitamins to your diet. Make a list of foods that are a source of vitamins.

Chapter 36	**WORDS OF THE WEEK:** endure, perpetuate, perseverance, **persevere**, persist, persistence, prevail, strive
DAY 1	USAGE Introduce and define *persevere*. In what situations might you need to *persevere*?
DAY 2 p. 106	WORD FAMILIES Write *persevere*, *perseverance*, and *persevered* on the board. What base word is common to these words?
DAY 3 p. 107	COMPARE/CONTRAST How are *persevere* and *persist* alike? Different?
DAY 4 p. 108	CONTEXT CLUES What are the clues to the meaning of *persevere* in the sentence? *The tortoise wins the race because she never stops. She perseveres.*
DAY 5	WORD PARTS Write *persevere* and *severe*. What is the base word? Use the base word *severe* to list as many words as possible, by adding prefixes or suffixes.

Weekly Instructional Plans T11

Activities

Word Wall

Create a Word Wall for students to use as a resource for reading, writing, and vocabulary development. Each week, add five or more words to the wall. These words can come from various sources: **Vocabulary Power** words, students' reading, or commonly misspelled words from students' writing. Write the words on cards and arrange them alphabetically. You may want to color-code the word cards. For example, use pink for nouns, yellow for verbs, and white for high-frequency words. Add each word to the Word Wall after it has been introduced. Continually add, take away, and move words around on the wall, as needed for instruction.

Word Wall Activities

- Have students regularly read all the words on the Word Wall.
- Have a word hunt. Ask students to look for categories of words, such as adjectives, plurals, or words with a common suffix. Categories can also be things like ways to move, baseball words, or math words.
- Say sentences with a blank for a missing word. Tell students the category of word that fits in the blank, such as a noun or a verb. Students choose words from the wall that fit the sentence.
- Dictate sentences using words from the Word Wall. Students can also create sentences with the words.

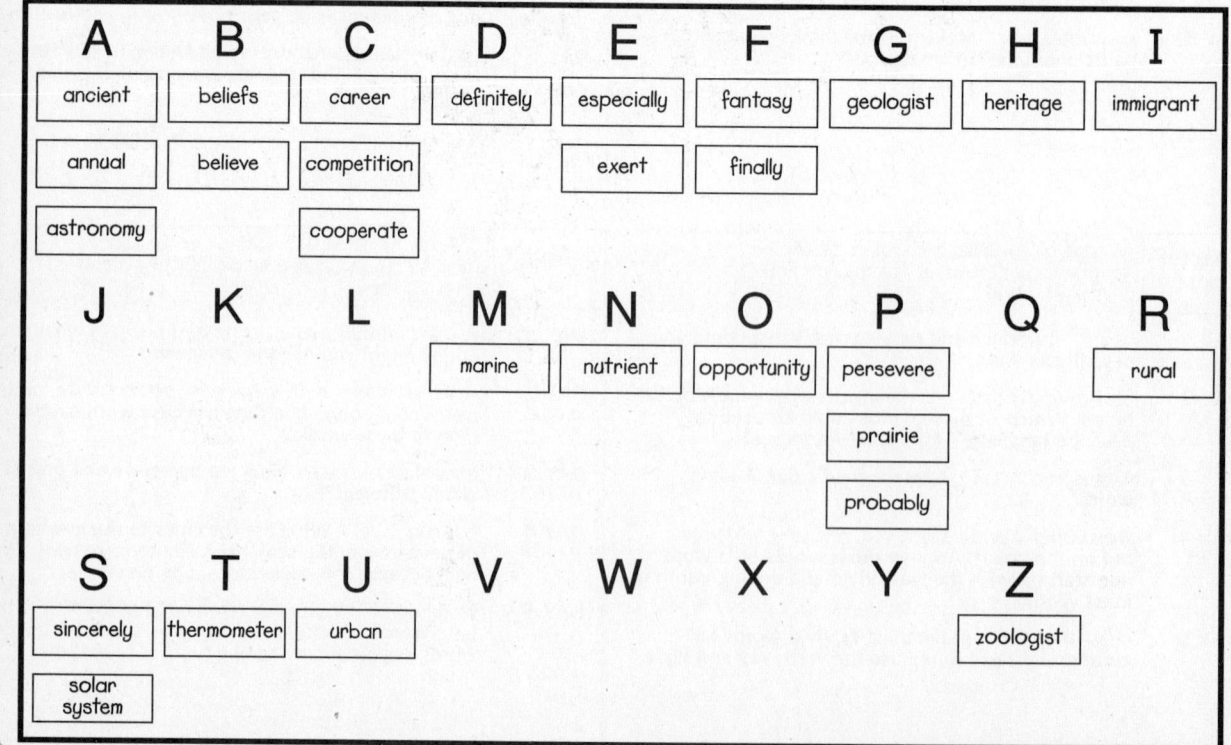

T12 Vocabulary Power Teacher's Guide

Journal

Students can choose words from the weekly word lists to record in a word bank in their Writer's Journals. They might keep lists of verbs, adjectives, and adverbs to refer to when they write. Students can also do activities like these to extend their understanding of the words:
- illustrate the words
- write sentences or stories
- add more words that are related
- write synonyms and antonyms
- form plurals
- add endings to the words, such as *ed* or *ing*
- add other words that can be formed with the same base word

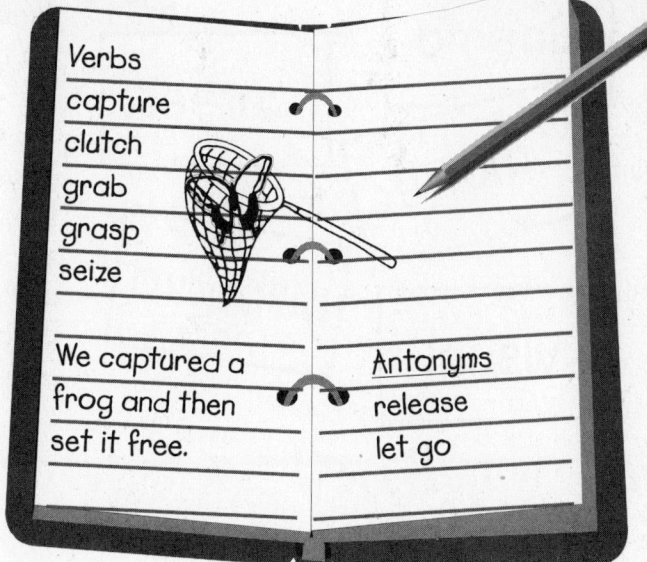

Say It!

I am eating a luscious lunch!

To help students make the **Vocabulary Power** words part of their vocabulary, challenge them to use the words in everyday situations in the classroom. Make it fun! Encourage them to try out the new words. You may want to organize students into teams and have a chart or some other way to keep track of how often the words are used in a week.

Word Cards

Vocabulary Power word cards can be found on pages T25–T48. Duplicate and distribute the cards. You may want to have students store the cards in a large self-seal baggy. They can write the meaning or an example sentence on the back of the card to help them learn the word. Students can use them as flash cards to read through and to quiz each other. The word cards can also be used in word sorts and in a variety of games.

Word Sorts

In word sorting, students match or categorize words according to features such as sound, pattern, meaning, or use. For example, words might be sorted according to part of speech, prefixes or suffixes, number of syllables, or similarities in meaning. Students may use their word cards to do an open sort or a closed sort.
- In an open sort, the student looks at a group of words and decides on the categories for sorting.
- In a closed sort, the teacher gives the categories and models the sorting procedure.

Concentration

Have partners put their sets of word cards together face down. Each player takes a turn turning over two cards. If the cards match, the player keeps the cards and takes another turn. If the cards do not match, the cards are turned face down and the other player takes a turn.

Word Ladders

Put the words face down in a pile. Have a player choose a card, read it, and say the meaning or use it in a sentence. If the meaning or sentence is correct, the word card is placed in the bottom pocket of a pocket chart or on a tabletop near the edge. The same player chooses another word and repeats the activity, placing the word above the other card. He or she tries to make as tall a ladder as possible. Challenge students to see who can make the tallest ladder and to read up and down each other's ladders.

sputter
flicker
quiver
shiver
flutter

Guess the Word

For this game, students need a set of word cards for words that they have studied. The object of the game is to guess a word from as few clues as possible. Organize students into two teams. Students on each team play in pairs. One player in each pair is the clue giver, and one is the guesser. The clue giver draws a word card and gives his or her partner clues until the partner names the correct word. A scorekeeper writes down the number of clues that were needed. Play alternates between the teams. When all word cards have been used, the team with fewer clues wins.

Act It Out!

Have a volunteer or small group choose a **Vocabulary Power** word to act out. The rest of the students guess the word.

Getting Specific

Provide a grid similiar to the following for students to complete individually or with a partner. Students might begin with a general concept such as *store*, *vehicle*, or *place*.

General	Less General	Specific	More Specific
food	vegetable	green, leafy vegetable	lettuce

Illustrate Homphones

Have students write and illustrate phrases that use homophones—for example, *the dear deer, hear it here, thrown from the throne.*

Idiom Search

Students can look in advertisements for examples of idioms and figurative language. Invite them to share their examples and tell whether the meaning of each is clear.

Synonyms and Antonyms

- Prepare a set of word or phrase pairs for students to illustrate. Students might illustrate each pair on opposite sides of an index card and ask a classmate or family member to guess the antonym pair.

    cloudy—sunny

    polite—rude

- Provide a list of word pairs and a grid with headings. Students place word pairs in the appropriate columns.

Same	Opposite	Go Together	Not Related
big–large	hot–cold	green–grass	guitar–north

Writing Palindromes

Challenge students to write their own palindromes. (See the examples on page T21.) Point out that some words form other words when spelled backwards (for example, *but*, *not*, *spot*, *won*). Tell students that they can use any numbers (for example, 101) as well as words.

Graphic Organizers

Semantic Map

Semantic mapping is a concept development approach to vocabulary instruction. It shows the organization and relationship of concepts in a visual way.

The steps in the process:

Brainstorm   1. Brainstorm and list words related to a concept or topic.
Classify   2. Analyze ideas to decide what categories seem to be represented.
Map   3. Construct the map to visually represent the relationship between the ideas. Add labels to the map to further the classification practice.

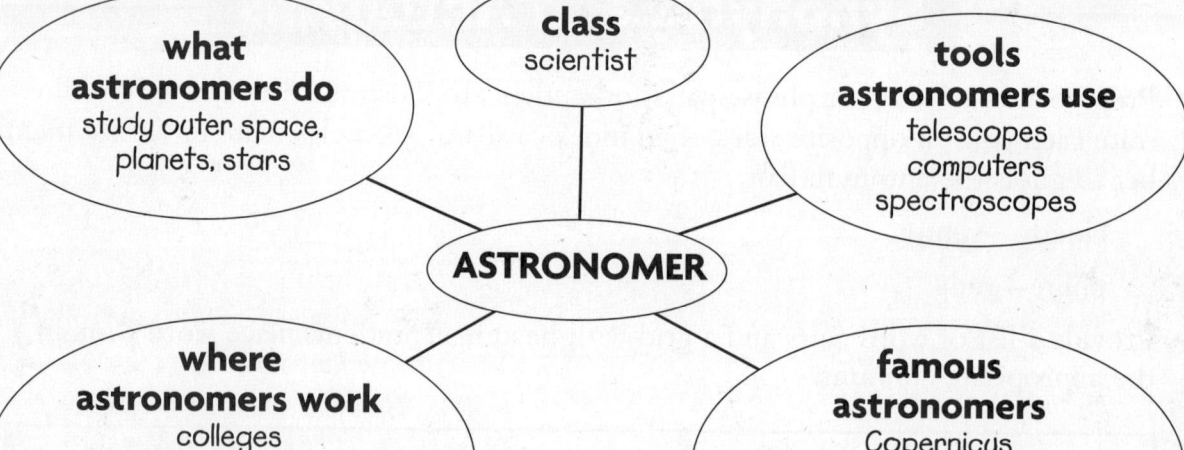

Word Web

Word Webs are collections of related words. Using a center space and web strands, students generate structurally or conceptually related words.

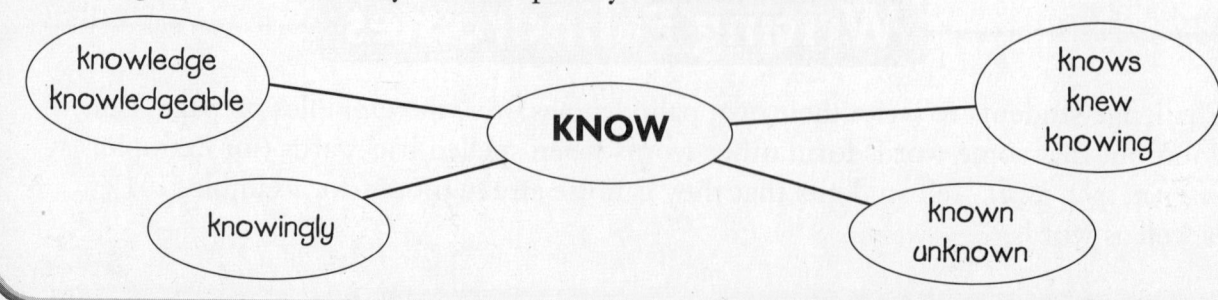

T18   Vocabulary Power Teacher's Guide

Synonym Ranking

Students compare and contrast related words to develop a greater sensitivity to meaning. They place the words on a continuum. The sequence can be based on intensity, size, chronology, or position.

Words: cool   hot   lukewarm   boiling   freezing   tepid   cold

boiling   freezing
_____
hottest   *coldest*

Word Definition Map

Students can use this strategy, developed by Schwartz and Raphael (1985), to acquire new vocabulary independently as they read. Students create the map by organizing information from text, background knowledge, and glossaries and dictionaries.

A word definition map includes three categories of information, as shown by the questions below.

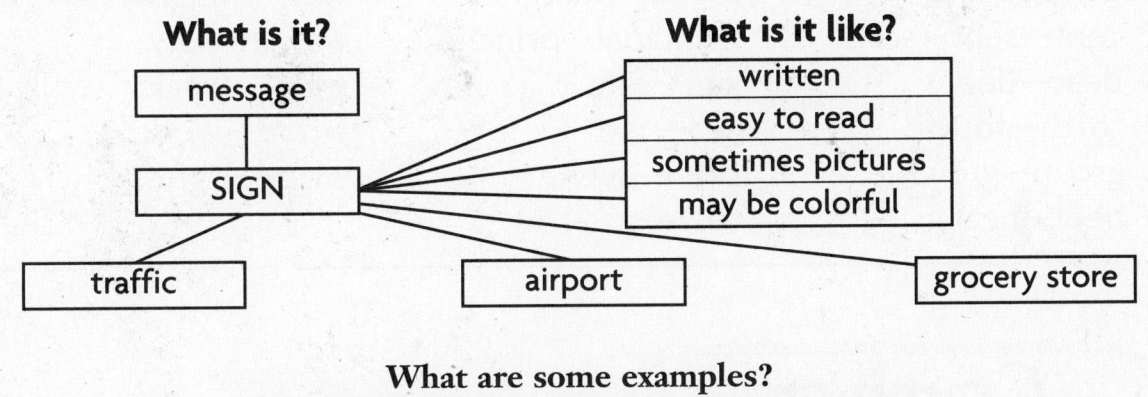

What are some examples?

Word Association Tree

Students can use branching diagrams to extend their understanding of words. Students begin with a target word and use what they know and what they can learn to produce two branches from this word "root." They label the branches with words they associate with the target word. For each meaning-associated word, two more branches are drawn. Students continue to brainstorm words branching off from the related words.

Word Lists

Common Homophones

ate—eight
base—bass
be—bee
bear—bare
beat—beet
blue—blew
bored—board
bow—bough
break—brake
buy—by
cell—sell
cent—sent—scent
dear—deer
forth—fourth
groan—grown
heel—heal
here—hear
hour—our
made—maid
mail—male
new—knew
no—know
one—won
pain—pane
peace—piece
peek—peak
plane—plain
principal—principle
sail—sale
sea—see
seen—scene
sew—so—sow
sight—site—cite
some—sum
sore—soar
stare—stair
steal—steel
sun—son
tail—tale
their—there—they're
through—threw
to—too—two
wait—weight
way—weigh
week—weak
wood—would
write—right

Common Homographs

alternate
associate
bass
bow
close
conflict
content
contrast
decrease
dove
elaborate
entrance
estimate
excuse
graduate
import
increase
lead
live
minute
object
present
produce
progress
protest
read
record
separate
tear
use
wind
wound

Idioms and Figurative Language

hold your horses
hit the ceiling
don't beat around the bush
all ears
at the end of one's rope
eyes bigger than your stomach
get going
go to bat for someone
let the cat out of the bag
play it by ear

smell a rat
spill the beans
straw that broke the camel's back
under the weather
give someone the cold shoulder
bury your head in sand
in one ear and out the other
straight from the horse's mouth
thinking cap
turn over a new leaf

Palindromes

Mom
Dad
noon
level
peep
did
solos
civic
refer
deed
Anna

Bob
tot
eye
Never odd or even
Step on no pets.
Madam, I'm Adam.
Ma handed Edna ham.
Stressed desserts
A man, a plan, a canal, Panama!
Did Hannah say as Hannah did?

Greek Roots

Root	Meaning	Examples
cycle	circle	bicycle, unicycle, cyclone
graph	write	graphite, telegraph, autograph
meter	measure	thermometer, diameter
micr	small	microscope, microbe
phon	sound	phonograph, symphony
photo	light	photograph, photosynthesis

Latin Roots

Root	Meaning	Examples
act	do	transact, actor, react
aud	hear	audible, audience, audition
dict	speak	dictate, predict
loc	place	locale, locate
ped	foot	pedal, pedestrian
port	carry	transport, portable

Words for Said

added	exclaimed	noted	reminded
admitted	explained	objected	repeated
announced	fretted	observed	replied
answered	fussed	ordered	reported
argued	gasped	pleaded	requested
asked	groaned	pointed out	responded
babbled	growled	praised	roared
begged	grumbled	proclaimed	sang
bellowed	hinted	promised	scoffed
blurted out	howled	pronounced	scolded
boasted	inquired	proposed	screamed
boomed	insisted	protested	shouted
bragged	instructed	questioned	snapped
called	interrupted	quipped	spoke
cautioned	jeered	quoted	stammered
challenged	joked	raged	stated
chanted	kidded	read	stressed
chimed in	mentioned	recalled	told
commented	moaned	recited	urged
cried	murmured	recounted	whispered
droned	muttered	reflected	yelled
echoed	named	remarked	

Words for Went

bounced	hopped	shuffled
chased	hurried	skated
clambered	jogged	skidded
climbed	journeyed	skipped
crawled	leaped	slid
crept	left town	sped
danced	limped	staggered
darted	marched	stepped
departed	migrated	strayed
disappeared	moved	streaked
drove	plunged	strode
embarked	pranced	strolled
emigrated	rambled	strutted
filed	ran	swarmed
flew	rode	swept
fled	rose	swooped
floated	rushed	traveled
flowed	sailed	trotted
fluttered	sank	walked
galloped	scampered	wandered
glided	scrambled	whizzed
hobbled	scurried	

employment	specialization
livelihood	vocation
occupation	auctioneer
position	engineer
profession	jeweler
pursuit	mountaineer

photographer	exactly
pioneer	inaccurately
senator	nearly
volunteer	precisely
approximately	roughly
barely	virtually

budget	resources
business	spending
credit	arts
currency	civilization
debt	cuisine
economy	culture

ethnicity	biography
folklore	diary
language	interview
society	journal
autobiography	memoir
autograph	photograph

anatomy	skeleton
composition	structure
form	alpine
frame	aquatic
framework	arctic
mold	arid

habitat	order
subterranean	organization
temperate	progression
tropical	sequel
arrangement	sequence
continuous	subsequent

geographer	seismograph
geologist	volcanic
gravity	coastal
magma	marine
petroleum	mariner
sediment	maritime

Word Cards T31

nautical	flower
naval	progress
oceanic	prosper
submarine	succeed
blossom	survive
flourish	thrive

acrylic	palette
bristle	subject
canvas	fable
easel	fiction
impression	folktale
landscape	literature

myth	happenstance
narrative	occasion
nonfiction	occurrence
poetry	opportunity
chance	probability
circumstance	serendipity

choreograph	orchestrate
choreographer	perform
compose	carnival
conduct	carousel
conductor	gilded
entertain	melodious

musical	pedestal
ornate	pedestrian
rotating	plaque
whirligig	podiatrist
dedication	scaffold
monument	sculpt

ambiance	surrounding
atmosphere	vapor
climate	aster
oxygen	asterisk
ozone	asteroid
smog	astral

astrodome	extra-sensitive
astronaut	extraordinary
astronautics	nocturnal
astronomer	ocular
auditory	olfactory
diurnal	perception

arboretum	greenhouse
botanical	vegetation
botanist	abrasion
botany	coastline
flora	erosion
foliage	glacier

gravel	devastate
wear	obliterate
weathering	refurbish
windswept	renovate
demolish	restore
destroy	revive

boulevard	subway
civic	urban
downtown	ancestor
metropolitan	genealogy
municipal	heredity
skyscraper	heritage

history	translate
inheritance	translucent
legacy	transmountain
origin	transoceanic
transatlantic	transparent
transcontinental	transport

aqueduct	sluice
canal	trough
drench	delta
hydrate	inlet
irrigate	meander
moisten	oasis

source	arachnid
tidal	crustacean
tributary	invertebrate
valley	mammal
amphibian	reptilian
amphibious	vertebrate

amusement	relaxation
diversion	repose
leisure	amateur
pastime	beginner
pleasure	dabbler
recreation	fledging

novice	emphatic
professional	picturesque
rookie	radiant
trainee	vibrant
colorful	vivacious
descriptive	vivid

competition	tournament
conflict	victor
contender	deficient
meet	essential
opponent	revitalize
rival	supplement

vigor	perseverance
vital	persevere
vitality	persist
vitamin	persistence
endure	prevail
perpetuate	strive

Vocabulary Power

Grade 4

Copyright © by Harcourt, Inc.

All rights reserved. No part of this publication may be reproduced or transmitted in any form or by any means, electronic or mechanical, including photocopy, recording, or any information storage and retrieval system, without permission in writing from the publisher.

Permission is hereby granted to individual teachers using the corresponding student's textbook or kit as the major vehicle for regular classroom instruction to photocopy complete student pages from this publication in classroom quantities for instructional use and not for resale.

Duplication of this work other than by individual classroom teachers under the conditions specified above requires a license. To order a license to duplicate this work in greater than classroom quantities, contact Customer Service, Harcourt, Inc., 6277 Sea Harbor Drive, Orlando, Florida 32887-6777. Telephone: 1-800-225-5425. Fax: 1-800-874-6418 or 407-352-3445.

HARCOURT and the Harcourt Logo are trademarks of Harcourt, Inc.

Printed in the United States of America

ISBN 0-15-320610-1

3 4 5 6 7 8 9 10 082 2003 2002 2001

Table of Contents

CHAPTER

1
- Connotation/Denotation 1
- Suffixes 2
- Analogies; Compare/Contrast 3

2
- Suffixes 4
- Multiple-Meaning Words 5
- Dictionary 6

3
- Explore Word Meanings 7
- Suffixes 8
- Gradient Analysis 9

4
- Classify/Categorize 10
- Context Clues 11
- Compare/Contrast 12

5
- Content-Area Words 13
- Word Families 14
- Related Words 15

6
- Classify/Categorize 16
- Greek Roots 17
- Compare/Contrast 18

7
- Multiple-Meaning Words 19
- Content-Area Words 20
- Synonyms 21

8
- Classify/Categorize 22
- Analogies 23
- Word Families 24

9
- Context Clues 25
- Explore Word Meaning 26
- Synonyms 27

10
- Classify/Categorize 28
- Compare/Contrast 29
- Suffixes 30

11
- Explore Word Meaning 31
- Analogies 32
- Content-Area Words 33

12
- Explore Word Meanings 34
- Homophones and Homographs 35
- Connotation/Denotation 36

CHAPTER

13
- Content-Area Words 37
- Multiple-Meaning Words 38
- Analogies 39

14
- Explore Word Meaning 40
- Analogies 41
- Antonyms 42

15
- Synonyms 43
- Classify/Categorize 44
- Words in Context; Dictionary 45

16
- Classify/Categorize 46
- Suffixes 47
- Compare/Contrast 48

17
- Related Words 49
- Context Clues 50
- Compare/Contrast 51

18
- Related Words 52
- Greek and Latin Roots 53
- Explore Word Meaning 54

19
- Explore Word Meaning 55
- Multiple-Meaning Words 56
- Classify/Categorize 57

20
- Greek and Latin Roots 58
- Compare/Contrast 59
- Related Words 60

21
- Related Words 61
- Prefixes 62
- Analogies 63

22
- Context Clues 64
- Classify/Categorize 65
- Compare/Contrast 66

23
- Content-Area Words 67
- Analogies 68
- Synonyms and Antonyms 69

24
- Synonyms 70
- Word Families 71
- Explore Word Meaning 72

CHAPTER

25 Compare/Contrast 73
Compound Words; Coined Words 74
Connotation/Denotation 75

26 Explore Word Meaning 76
Context Clues 77
Classify/Categorize 78

27 Context Clues 79
Explore Word Meaning 80
Word Families 81

28 Related Words 82
Word Families 83
Context Clues 84

29 Related Words 85
Compare/Contrast 86
Analogies 87

30 Classify/Categorize 88
Word Families 89
Compare/Contrast 90

31 Rhyming Words 91
Synonyms 92
Connotation/Denotation 93

32 Compare/Contrast 94
Euphemisms 95
Antonyms; Colloquialisms 96

33 Classify/Categorize 97
Words in Context 98
Word Lines 99

34 Analogies; Rhyming Words 100
Word Families 101
Classify/Categorize 102

35 Analogies 103
Latin Roots 104
Context Clues 105

36 Word Families 106
Compare/Contrast 107
Context Clues 108

GLOSSARY 109

Name _____

CONNOTATION/DENOTATION

The words in italic type in the questions below all have meanings similar to *occupation*. Each has its own connotation, or slightly different shade of meaning. Think about the way these words are used as you answer each question. *Responses will vary. Accept reasonable responses.*

1. Would you rather have an *occupation* or a *profession*? Why?

   _____

   _____

2. What title might a person have if he or she holds a high *position* in a company?

   _____

   _____

3. *Livelihood* is like *pursuit* except that _____

   _____

   _____

4. Would you expect to earn more money if you had a *job* or a *specialization*? Explain why.

   _____

   _____

5. *Vocation* often has the connotation that a job matches someone's personality. What vocation would suit a person who loves numbers and mathematics?

   _____

   _____

Vocabulary Power

Name _____

SUFFIXES

When you add *-tion* or *-ment* to a verb, you form a noun that means "the act of" or "something that." Add suffixes to each of the following words. Then write what the new word means. The first one is done for you.

1. occupy + tion = __occupation__. __something that keeps you occupied__

2. specialize + tion = __specialization__. __Responses will vary. Accept reasonable responses.__

3. educate + tion = __education__. _____

4. entertain + ment = __entertainment__. _____

5. employ + ment = __employment__. _____

6. define + tion = __definition__. _____

7. introduce + tion = __introduction__. _____

8. invite + tion = __invitation__. _____

9. inform + tion = __information__. _____

10. enjoy + ment = __enjoyment__. _____

Name _____

ANALOGIES

An analogy is made of two pairs of words. The words in each pair are related to each other in the same way. Choose a word that completes each analogy. Responses will vary. Accept reasonable responses.

1. *Livelihood* is to *profession* as *happy* is to _____.

2. *Directors* are to *movies* as *editors* are to _____.

3. *Stories* are to *writers* as _____ are to *webmasters*.

4. *Position* is to *manager* as *vocation* is to _____.

5. *Mail carriers* are to *letters* as *chefs* are to _____.

6. *Pursuit* is to *farming* as *hobby* is to _____.

7. *Musician* is to *guitarist* as *color* is to _____.

8. *Airplane* is to *ship* as *sky* is to _____.

COMPARE AND CONTRAST

To compare two items, tell how they are alike. To contrast, tell how they are different. Accept reasonable responses.

1. occupation, hobby

   Compare: _____

   Contrast: _____

2. specialization, livelihood

   Compare: _____

   Contrast: _____

3. sergeant, general

   Compare: _____

   Contrast: _____

Vocabulary Power

Name _____

SUFFIXES

▶ When added to a noun or verb, the suffixes *-eer*, *-er*, and *-or* often stand for "one who." Complete the following sentences with a word from the box. Then write a definition for the word, using the example provided.

| auctioneer | mountaineer | volunteer | jeweler |
| pioneer | engineer | senator | photographer |

1. The <u>photographer</u> used a camera with a powerful lens to take pictures of the lions. <u>one who takes photographs</u>

2. Long ago, trains used steam engines that were powered by coal. The train driver was called an ____engineer____.
   <u>one who operates an engine</u>

3. The ____auctioneer____ called for higher bids on the antique furniture.
   <u>one who runs an auction</u>

4. As an experienced ____mountaineer____, Joel planned to climb Mt. McKinley. <u>one who climbs mountains</u>

5. The voters re-elected the ____senator____ to office because of the work he had done for his state.
   <u>one who is elected to the Senate</u>

6. Mrs. Green had her broken earring repaired by the ____jeweler____.
   <u>one who makes or repairs jewelry</u>

▶ Write the word defined below. Then write a sentence using the word.

7. someone who offers to work without receiving payment ____volunteer____
   <u>Sentences will vary. Accept reasonable responses.</u>

8. someone who settled in an area before others did ____pioneer____

4 Unit 1 • Chapter 2   Vocabulary Power

Name _____

MULTIPLE-MEANING WORDS

Read each sentence below. Then circle the letter next to the correct meaning of each underlined word.

1. My neighbor is a <u>volunteer</u> at the hospital.
   - **(A)** a person who works without pay
   - **B** to give or offer readily

2. The scientist hopes to <u>engineer</u> a new type of electric motor.
   - **A** a person who builds machines
   - **(B)** to create and make plans for something

3. The United States of America <u>pioneered</u> space travel.
   - **(A)** to be the first to do something
   - **B** a person who does something before anyone else

4. The fire <u>chief</u> gives orders to the firefighters.
   - **(A)** the leader of a group
   - **B** most important, main

5. The team of <u>mountaineers</u> planned to hike in the Himalayas.
   - **(A)** people who climb or live on a mountain
   - **B** climbs mountains for enjoyment

6. My puppy likes to sit in my <u>lap</u>.
   - **(A)** the front part of the body between the waist and the knees of a seated person
   - **B** one time around or over the entire length of something

7. Brad found an injured sparrow and will <u>nurse</u> it back to health.
   - **A** a person who takes care of the sick
   - **(B)** to take care of someone or something that is ill

8. I am learning how to <u>iron</u> my own shirts.
   - **(A)** to press clothes to remove wrinkles
   - **B** a hard metal

Vocabulary Power

Name _____

DICTIONARY

▶ For each word below, circle the letter of the pair of guide words that could be at the top of a dictionary page containing the word.

1. volunteer
   A vision/vocabulary
   B vitamin/volcano
   (C) voile/votary
   D visitor/voice

2. photographer
   (F) phonics/phrase
   G pharmacy/photocopy
   H photography/piano
   J photon/physics

3. senator
   A school/semester
   B season/senate
   (C) section/separate
   D saddle/select

4. jeweler
   (F) jellyfish/jewelry
   G jersey/jewel
   H jigsaw/juggle
   J justice/kale

5. auctioneer
   A attack/auction
   B aunt/awake
   C audible/awful
   (D) auburn/avenue

6. occupation
   F occupy/offer
   (G) obvious/ocean
   H oak/occupant
   J occur/odd

▶ Now, write the guide words you might find on the page that contains these words. Accept reasonable responses.

7. equipment _____

8. chief _____

9. sandwich _____

10. livelihood _____

11. engineer _____

12. museum _____

6   Unit 1 • Chapter 2   Vocabulary Power

Name _____

EXPLORE WORD MEANINGS

Think about the meaning of the underlined words. Answer each question.

Possible responses are given.

1. Wilbur had <u>barely</u> enough time to catch the bus. At right, draw a picture of Wilbur on his way to the bus stop.

   Picture should represent a boy in a hurry.

   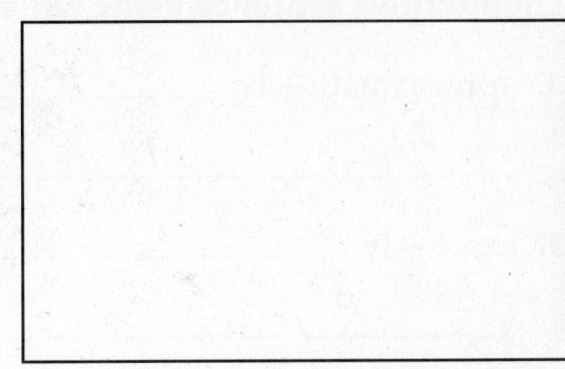

2. Although there was a chill in the air, it was <u>virtually</u> spring. What season was it?

   It was the end of winter.

3. Jeb has two quarters, a dime, and three pennies. He wants to buy some apple juice that costs 65 cents. To have <u>precisely</u> the right amount of money, what does Jeb need?

   Jeb needs two pennies or two cents.

4. The strength of the bridge was measured <u>inaccurately</u>. Explain how you would feel about traveling across it.

   Possible response: I would be afraid that the bridge might collapse.

5. The park rangers reported seeing <u>approximately</u> 50 deer. What number could there have been?

   Accept responses between 45 and 55.

   If they reported <u>nearly</u> 50 deer, how might your answer be different?

   Accept responses between 45 and 49.

6. Brenda has one dollar. Her notebook costs <u>exactly</u> 82 cents. How much change will she receive?

   Brenda will receive 18 cents change.

7. Replace the underlined word with a synonym:
   The box contains <u>roughly</u> 95 raisins.

   Possible responses: approximately, about, more or less

Vocabulary Power   Unit 1 • Chapter 3   7

Name _____

SUFFIXES

Write the word that is created when *-ly* is added to the adjectives below. Then write a sentence using the new word.

1. approximate + ly = _____ approximately _____

   Accept reasonable responses. _____

2. exact + ly = _____ exactly _____

   _____

3. perfect + ly = _____ perfectly _____

   _____

4. near + ly = _____ nearly _____

   _____

5. quick + ly = _____ quickly _____

   _____

6. inaccurate + ly = _____ inaccurately _____

   _____

7. strong + ly = _____ strongly _____

   _____

8. Make your own *-ly* word and use it in a sentence.

   _____ + _____ = _____

   _____

   _____

Name _____

GRADIENT ANALYSIS

On the lines provided, arrange each group of words in the order asked for.

From least accurate to most accurate: precisely, virtually, barely, roughly

___barely___   ___roughly___   ___virtually___   ___precisely___

From smallest to largest: small, tiny, average, minute

___minute___   ___tiny___   ___small___   ___average___

From January to November: spring, autumn, summer, winter

___winter___   ___spring___   ___summer___   ___autumn___

From longest to shortest: yard, foot, mile, inch

___mile___   ___yard___   ___foot___   ___inch___

Vocabulary Power

Name _____

CLASSIFY/CATEGORIZE

Cross out the word in each group that doesn't belong. Then name the category on the line. The first one is done for you. Add your own word to each category. *Possible responses are given.*

1. farming   manufacturing   fishing   ~~walking~~
   _____ types of work; building _____

2. business   commerce   trade   ~~leisure~~
   names for business; market, exchange

3. budget   income   ~~factories~~   expenses
   words to do with keeping track of money; receipts, records

4. ~~profit~~   debt   loan   credit
   words to do with borrowing money; owe, lend

5. economics   ~~ecosystem~~   economy   economist
   words with the same root; economical

6. capital   currency   cash   ~~spending~~
   words that mean "money"; principal, dollars

7. resources   materials   supplies   ~~antiques~~
   things you need to earn money; market, customers

8. ~~factories~~   farms   orchards   crops
   agriculture, or growing things on the land; harvest, plough

Name _____

CONTEXT CLUES

Read each sentence below. Use context clues to figure out the meaning of each underlined word. Circle the letter of the correct meaning.

1. Jim wanted to know more about his business's <u>economy</u>. He wanted to know how its income was managed.
   A customers and suppliers
   B phone number and address
   (C) management of money
   D largest size of a product

2. Natural <u>resources</u> such as oil and timber should be used carefully.
   F forests
   G merchandise
   (H) supplies
   J gasoline

3. I worked out a <u>budget</u> so that I can buy a new bike.
   A an exercise plan
   B a method of getting something finished
   C a savings account
   (D) a plan for saving and spending

4. Telephones and e-mail are methods of <u>communicating</u> quickly.
   F transporting goods
   (G) sharing information
   H cutting the amount of time
   J following directions

5. Kevin and Kyle went into <u>business</u> together. They opened a pizza parlor.
   (A) a venture to earn a living
   B no one else's concern
   C an errand
   D a difficult task

Vocabulary Power   Unit 1 • Chapter 4   11

Name _____

COMPARE AND CONTRAST

Complete the following statements. Responses will vary. Accept reasonable responses.

1. *Tokens* are like *currency* except that _____
_____

2. *Borrowing* is like *debt* because _____
_____

3. *Spending* is like a *budget* except that _____
_____

4. A *supermarket* is like a *restaurant* because _____
_____

5. A *bank account* is like a *piggy bank* except that _____
_____

6. *Libraries* are like *bookstores* but _____
_____

7. *Assembled* is like *manufactured* because _____
_____

8. *Crops* are like *livestock* because _____
_____

9. A *manager* is like a *principal* because _____
_____

10. An *employee* is like a *student* but _____
_____

12 Unit 1 • Chapter 4   Vocabulary Power

Name _____

CONTENT-AREA WORDS

Read the words in the box. Then answer the questions below.

| civilization | arts | language | culture |
| cuisine | society | folklore | ethnicity |

1. Which four words describe people as a group?

   culture, civilization, society, ethnicity

2. Which word is a label for the following:

   jazz, pantomime, cinema, sculpture? _____arts_____

   Give another example that fits this category. _Examples will vary._

3. Which word deals with the way people communicate? _language_

   Name two or three other words that belong in this group. _____

4. Legends, myths, and tall tales are examples of _____folklore_____.

   Give examples of this. _____

5. The foods people eat and the manner in which they are prepared are

   related to _____cuisine_____.

   Name some dishes from a particular culture. _____

Vocabulary Power   Unit 1 • Chapter 5   13

Name _____

WORD FAMILIES

▶ Word families are made up of words that share the same root or base word. Read each set of words. Write the base word that the words in each set have in common.

1. acculturate, culturist, cultural _____culture_____
2. civilization, uncivilized, civility _____civil_____
3. society, socialization, antisocial _____social_____
4. befriend, friendliness, friendship _____friend_____
5. folktale, folk song, folksy, folklore _____folk_____
6. misuse, useful, used _____use_____
7. ethnicity, ethnical, multiethnic _____ethnic_____
8. celebration, celebrity, celebrated _____celebrate_____
9. servant, service, serving _____serve_____
10. apart, apartment, compartment _____part_____

▶ Now read each word below and think about its word family. Write two or three words that are related to each. *Possible responses are given.*

11. joy _____enjoy, enjoyable, joyful_____
12. child _____childhood, childish, children_____
13. warm _____warmth, warmly, warmest_____
14. happy _____happily, happiness, unhappy_____
15. art _____artist, artful, artistically_____
16. order _____reorder, disorderly, ordered_____

Name _____

RELATED WORDS

In the web below, fill in the boxes with words related to culture. Use the categories provided. Possible responses are given. Accept reasonable responses.

Language
English
Spanish
slang, dialect

The arts
movies, music, pottery,
sculpture, performers,
playwrights etc.

Culture

Cuisine
Types: Tex-Mex, Caribbean,
Italian
Dishes: barbecue, pizza,
apple pie

Folklore
folktales, tall tales
Paul Bunyan
The Three Billy Goats Gruff
storytelling

Vocabulary Power — Unit 1 • Chapter 5   15

Name _____

CLASSIFY/CATEGORIZE

Cross out the item which does not belong in the group. Then write a name for the category on the line provided. Add your own word that fits the category. Possible responses are given.

1. diary   journal   memoir   ~~news story~~
   _____ personal writing; letter _____

2. biography   ~~telephone~~   autobiography photograph
   _____ words with -graph; geography _____

3. ~~intermission~~ interview   quiz   interrogation
   _____ ways of asking questions; inquiry _____

4. textbook   novel   magazine   ~~motion picture~~
   _____ things you can read; menu _____

5. ~~typewriter~~ paper   pencil   pen
   _____ writing instruments; crayon _____

6. envelope   stamp   stationery   ~~reply~~
   _____ materials for writing a letter; computer _____

7. ~~reader~~   author   publisher   editor
   _____ people who work together to make books; typesetter, designer _____

8. jacket   ~~plot~~   spine   pages
   _____ parts of a book; title page _____

16 Unit 1 • Chapter 6   Vocabulary Power

Name _____

GREEK ROOTS

Many English words have been built using roots from ancient Greek. Read the roots and their meanings in the box below.

Greek root	auto	bio	graph	photo	tele
Meaning	self	life	written	light	at a distance

▶ Use what you already know about the following words and the information in the box to write a definition.

1. biography _the story of someone's life_

2. autobiography _the story of someone's own life, written by him- or herself_

3. autograph _written by self; signature_

▶ Fill in the blanks below by inserting or completing a word. Use the Greek roots above to help you.

4. A camera uses a special film which is exposed to the light for a very brief moment. The result is a ___photograph___.

5. A pilot is safely in the air and allows the plane to control itself. He puts it on ___auto___ pilot.

6. The ___tele___ vision allows us to see images such as movies that are broadcast from a distance.

7. Morse created a machine that sent written messages over a long distance. This was called a ___telegraph___, and it used an alphabet called Morse code.

8. Write your own words using the roots listed above.
Accept reasonable responses.

_____ _____

_____ _____

Vocabulary Power   Unit 1 • Chapter 6   17

Name _____

COMPARE AND CONTRAST

Read the word pairs below. Identify how they are alike and how they are different. The first one has been done for you. Accept reasonable responses.

1. **Saturday, Monday**

    Compare: Saturday and Monday are both days of the week.

    Contrast: Only Monday is a school day.

2. **biography, autobiography**

    Compare: _____

    Contrast: _____

3. **diary, memoir**

    Compare: _____

    Contrast: _____

4. **interview, test**

    Compare: _____

    Contrast: _____

5. **journal, logbook**

    Compare: _____

    Contrast: _____

6. Think of a pair of words that are alike in one way, but different in another. Write the pair, then compare and contrast them.

    _____, _____

    Compare: _____

    Contrast: _____

18   Unit 1 • Chapter 6   Vocabulary Power

Name _____

MULTIPLE-MEANING WORDS

Read each sentence and the definitions of the underlined word. Circle the letter that shows which way the word has been used.

1. After the fire all that remained of the old house was a roofless skeleton.
   - (A) the main columns and beams, without walls
   - B all the bones of a human body

2. The scientist's years of research laid the framework for his later inventions.
   - A the beginning of a house before walls are added
   - (B) a set of ideas from which to begin working

3. My sister made a pretty dessert by pouring fruit and gelatin into a heart-shaped mold.
   - (A) a pan which gives food a decorative shape
   - B a type of fungus found on damp or decaying surfaces

4. Bark and branches are part of the structure of most trees.
   - (A) what something is made of
   - B a building

5. The teenager was of a small frame and easily slipped through the railings to save the stranded puppy.
   - A an object used for displaying a photograph or painting
   - (B) the physical make-up of the body

6. The tailor uses a form so that his jackets are well-shaped.
   - (A) a model of the upper body used for fitting clothes
   - B a document with blank spaces to be filled with information

7. The composition of dark and light colors made the painting unusual.
   - A a written essay
   - (B) the way something is put together

8. In social studies we are learning about the anatomy of the government.
   - (A) the way that parts are organized
   - B the study of the parts of the body

Vocabulary Power

Name _____

CONTENT-AREA WORDS

▶ Each numbered group contains special vocabulary words for a certain topic or area of study. On the line provided, write the topic or area from the box that fits the list.

| drama | grammar | anatomy | music | social studies |

1. skeleton, muscles, veins _____ anatomy _____
2. actors, stage, costumes, plot _____ drama _____
3. nations, states, capitals, communities _____ social studies _____
4. composition, piano, treble clef _____ music _____
5. subject, predicate, sentence _____ grammar _____

| architecture | language arts | art | sports | mathematics |

6. subtraction, multiplication, division, patterns _____ mathematics _____
7. paints, brushes, easels, images _____ art _____
8. football, basketball, soccer, score _____ sports _____
9. framework, structure, base, foundation _____ architecture _____
10. speaking, listening, writing _____ language arts _____

▶ Choose two topic or category labels from either of the boxes above. List at least four additional words related to each of the labels you chose.

Label: _____   Label: _____

_____   _____

_____   _____

_____   _____

_____   _____

20 Unit 2 • Chapter 7   Vocabulary Power

Name _____

SYNONYMS

The words in the box are synonyms for one of the words in the web below. Write each one with its synonym. One has been done for you. Add your own synonyms to the web. Additional words will vary.

| form | character | mold | expression |
| identity | look | frame | individuality |

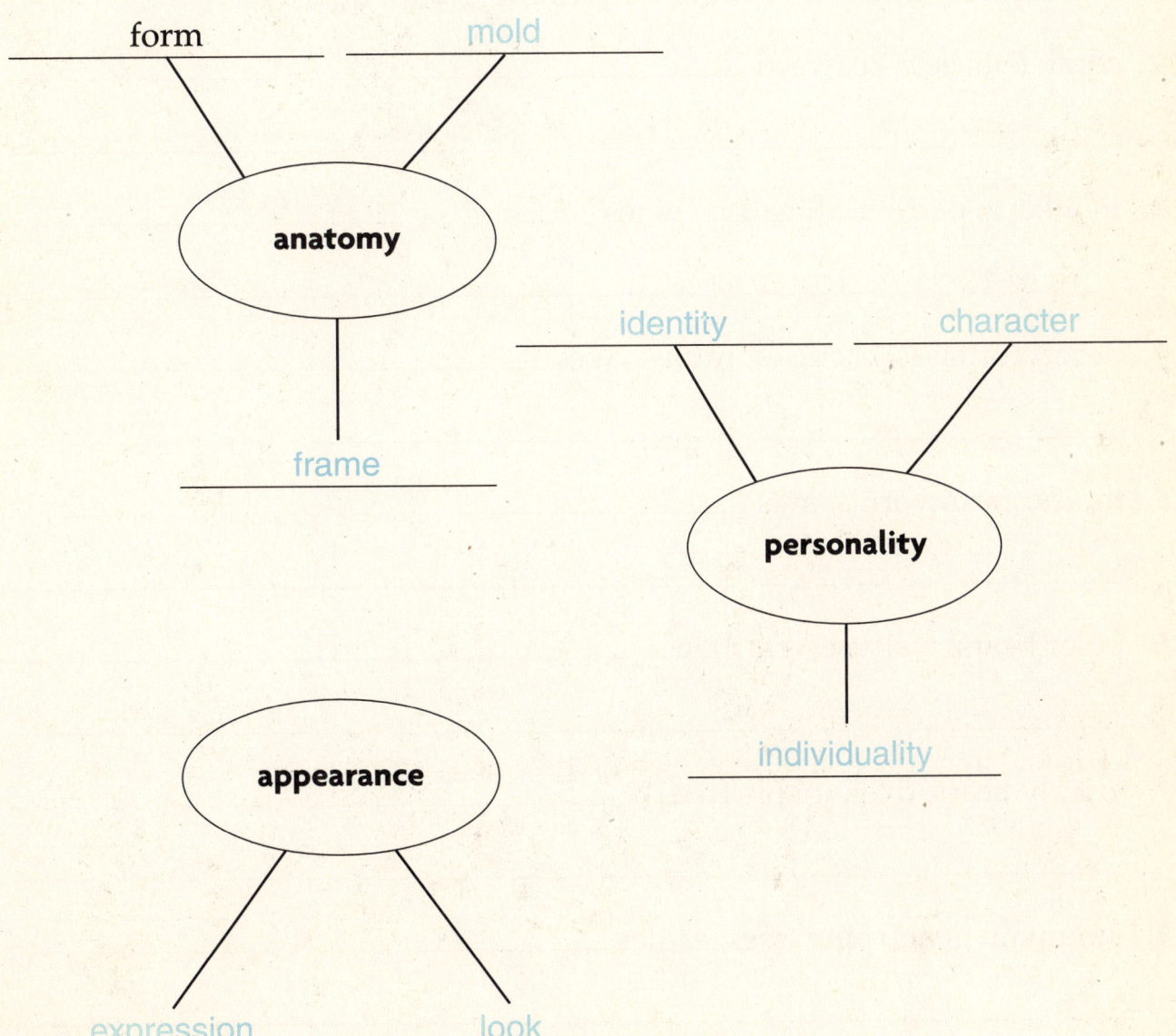

Vocabulary Power — Unit 2 • Chapter 7   21

Name _____

CLASSIFY/CATEGORIZE

Answer the following questions with a word from the box.

| aquatic | arctic | habitat | temperate |
| tropical | arid | alpine | subterranean |

1. Which word is a label for all the others? _____ habitat _____

Name the type of habitat in which you would find the following plants and animals. Add another inhabitant to the group.

2. coral, fish, eels, seaweed _____ aquatic _____

Responses will vary. Accept reasonable responses.

3. monkeys, parrots, alligators, vines _____ tropical _____

4. desert tortoises, cactuses, rattlesnakes _____ arid _____

5. moles, earthworms, ants _____ subterranean _____

6. polar bears, walruses, caribou _____ arctic _____

7. grizzly bears, deer, maple trees _____ temperate _____

8. mountain goats, pine trees, eagles _____ alpine _____

Name _____

ANALOGIES

▶ *Analogies* are made up of two pairs of words. Each pair is related in the same way. Complete the analogies below. The first one is done for you.

1. *Nest* is to *habitat* as _____oak_____ is to *tree*.
2. *Grass* is to *cows* as _____fish_____ are to *seals*.
3. *Fawn* is to _____deer_____ as *pup* is to *wolf*.
4. *Burrow* is to *woodchuck* as *den* is to _____bear_____.
5. *Arid* is to *desert* as _____humid/wet_____ is to *rain forest*.
6. *Jeep* is to *driving* as _____camera_____ is to *picture-taking*.
7. *Arctic* is to *tropical* as *east* is to _____west_____.
8. *Yes* is to *no* as *question* is to _____answer_____.
9. *Day* is to *week* as _____month_____ is to *year*.
10. *Alpine* is to _____mountains_____ as *coastal* is to *beach*.
11. *Mole* is to *subterranean* as _____fish_____ is to *aquatic*.
12. *Huge* is to *tiny* as *whale* is to _____housefly_____.

▶ **Now try this.** Responses will vary. Accept reasonable responses.

13. *Wolf* is to *dog* as _____ is to _____.
14. *Calf* is to *cow* as _____ is to _____.
15. *Frog* is to *amphibian* as _____ is to _____.
16. *Pasture* is to *meadows* as _____ is to _____.
17. *Camping* is to *tent* as _____ is to _____.

Vocabulary Power

Name _____

WORD FAMILIES

▶ Read the following groups of words. Look for the root or base word in the word family. Write the root or base word.

1. habitat, habitation, inhabit — habit
2. humanist, inhuman, human, humanitarian — human
3. planetary, planet, planetarium, planetoid — planet
4. coloration, colorfast, colorist — color
5. maximum, maxim, maximize, maximal — maxim
6. cracker, crackle, crackleware — crack
7. journalism, journalist, journalize — journal
8. worker, workmen, overworked — work
9. geology, geography, geometry, geode — geo
10. nonsense, sensitive, sensory, senseless — sense

▶ Write other words that belong to the same family as each of the following. Notice that some words may fit into more than one family. Possible responses are given.

11. aquatic — aqua, aquarium, aquamarine

12. subterranean

    sub — subway, subzero

    terr — terrain, Mediterranean, terrestrial

13. temperate

    temp — temperature, temper

    word part -ate — climate, moderate, animate

24 Unit 2 • Chapter 8   Vocabulary Power

Name _____

CONTEXT CLUES

▶ The words in the box are all related to the way in which things are arranged. They are each used in slightly different ways. Choose the word that best fits each sentence below.

sequence	arrangement	sequel	continuous
subsequent	organization	order	progression

1. A dictionary lists words in alphabetical _____order_____.

2. A 24-hour television channel offers viewers a _____continuous_____ broadcast.

3. The ushers seated the guests at the banquet according to the seating _____arrangement_____.

4. The movie was such a success that the following year the producers made a _____sequel_____ to it.

5. Chapter 6 and the _____subsequent_____ chapters in the unit all deal with fractions.

6. We are learning about the _____sequence_____ of events that led to the Revolutionary War.

7. The _____organization_____ of books at the library made it simple for patrons to find what they were looking for.

8. A steady _____progression_____ of spectators soon filled the stadium.

▶ Now try this. Write a word to complete each phrase.

9. numerical _____order_____   11. _____subsequent_____ pages

10. _____continuous_____ progress   12. _____arrangement_____ of flowers

Vocabulary Power   Unit 2 • Chapter 9   25

Name _____

EXPLORE WORD MEANINGS

Think about the meaning of the underlined words. Write answers to the questions.

1. Create a title for the <u>sequel</u> to "Morton Mouse Goes West."

   Responses will vary.

2. Starting with 20, list the four <u>subsequent</u> multiples of 10.

   30, 40, 50, 60

3. Write the following in numerical <u>order</u>, starting with the largest.

   12, 6, 24, 10, 16 _____ *24, 16, 12, 10, 6*

4. List in <u>sequence</u> the steps you take to prepare a snack. *Responses will vary.*

   a. _____ d. _____

   b. _____ e. _____

   c. _____ f. _____

5. What is the <u>arrangement</u> of desks in your classroom? Draw a rough sketch below.

Name _____

SYNONYMS

You can make word webs of synonyms. Write each word from the box on a line around its synonym. One word is written for you.

| constant | following | advancement | nonstop | set-up | arrangement |
| pattern | later | uninterrupted | progress | headway | succeeding |

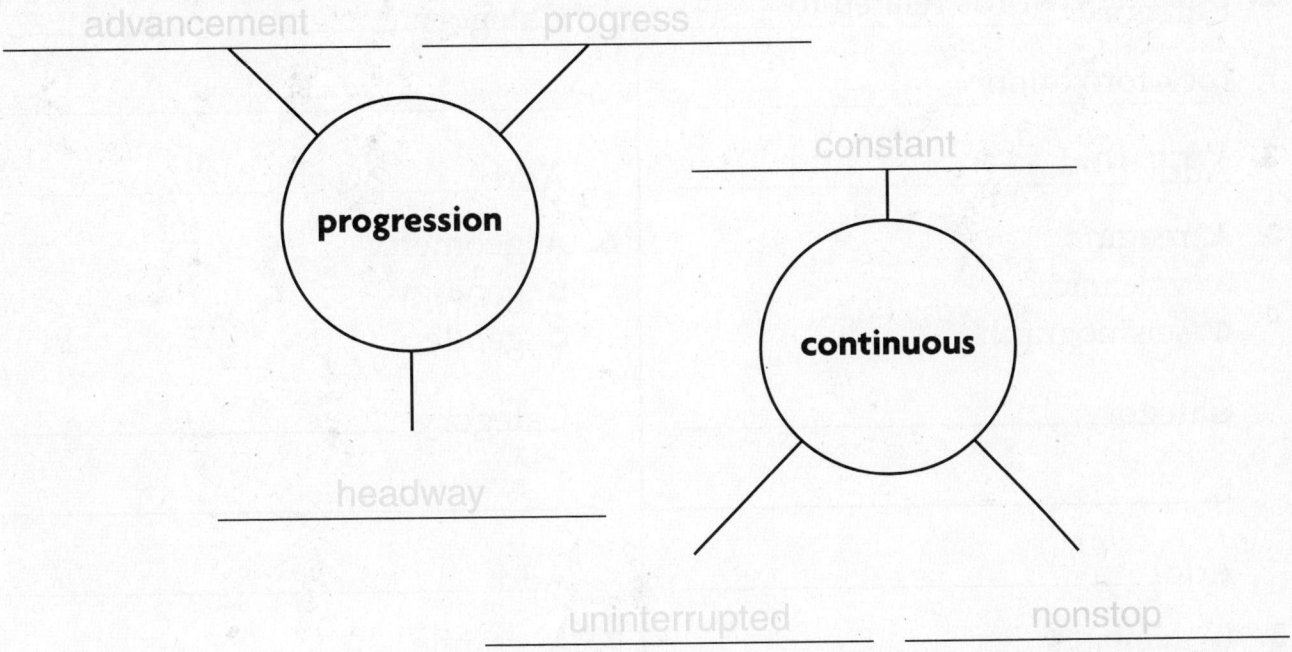

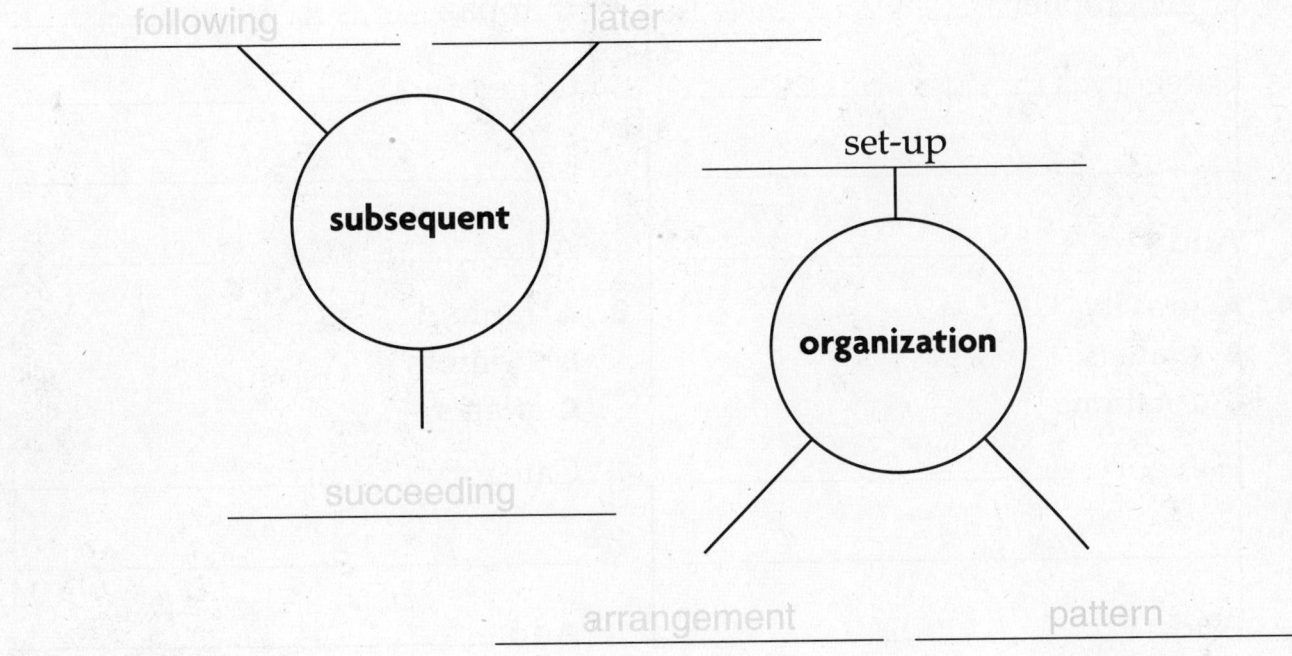

Vocabulary Power   Unit 2 • Chapter 9   27

Name _____

CLASSIFY/CATEGORIZE

Read the words in each list below. Label the category to which each group belongs. Then add another word to the list. The first has been done for you.

1. **A** sediment
   B deposits
   C rivers

   Category: words related to rock formation

   Add: sand

2. **A** magma
   B volcanic
   C seismograph

   Category: words related to volcanoes

   Add: _____

   Accept reasonable responses.

3. **A** geologist
   B photographer
   C geographer

   Category: occupations

   Add: _____

4. **A** gravity
   B planets
   C rotation

   Category: words related to the solar system

   Add: _____

5. **A** petroleum
   B fossils
   C minerals

   Category: things found in the earth

   Add: _____

6. **A** geometry
   B geology
   C geode

   Category: words with geo-

   Add: _____

7. **A** granite
   B quartz
   C topaz

   Category: rocks and minerals

   Add: _____

8. **A** faults
   B tremors
   C plates

   Category: earthquake words

   Add: _____

Vocabulary Power

Name _____

COMPARE AND CONTRAST

Complete the following sentences to describe how the two things named are alike or different. Responses will vary. Accept reasonable responses.

1. *Summer* is like *winter* because _____

2. *Petroleum* is like *gasoline* but _____

3. *Gravity* is like *glue* but _____

4. *Magma* is like *rock* except that _____

5. A *seismograph* is like a *speedometer* because _____

6. A *stalactite* is like a *stalagmite* but _____

7. *The Rockies* are like *the Andes* except that _____

8. A *diamond* is like a *ruby* because _____

9. *Iron* is like *gold* but _____

10. A *gemologist* is like a *geologist* because _____

Vocabulary Power

Name _____

SUFFIXES

Complete each sentence by adding a suffix to the word in parentheses. Choose one of the suffixes from the box below. Write the new word in the sentence.

Suffixes	Definition
-ed	an action or state in the past
-ic	related to, like
-ary	connected with, relating to
-ive	doing or tending to do something
-er, -ist	a person who does something

1. A _____geologist_____ is a person who studies the history of the earth. (**geology**)

2. Lava is _____melted_____ rock. (**melt**)

3. The firefighter's actions were _____heroic_____. (**hero**)

4. The fire _____burned_____ all night. (**burn**)

5. The _____volcanic_____ ash fell many miles from the eruption. (**volcano**)

6. Limestone is a _____sedimentary_____ rock, formed from small pieces of other rocks. (**sediment**)

7. A strong earthquake _____destroyed_____ the seaport. (**destroy**)

8. A _____geographer_____ studies the earth and its inhabitants. (**geography**)

Name _____

EXPLORE WORD MEANINGS

Write the word(s) from the box that best answer the following questions.

| marine | nautical | maritime | naval |
| mariner | oceanic | coastal | submarine |

1. Which words are related to the sea or ocean?

   __marine__ __nautical__ __maritime__ __naval__

   __mariner__ __oceanic__ __submarine__

2. Which word has to do with the land? __coastal__

3. Which words are related to the Latin root *mare*, which means "sea"?

   __marine__ __maritime__

   __mariner__ __submarine__

4. Which words come from the Latin root *navis* and the Greek root *naus*, which both mean "ship"? __naval__ __nautical__

5. In what kind of waters could you find a submarine? __oceanic__

6. Which word names a sailor, or person who navigates a ship?

   __mariner__

7. Which words could be used in relation to the armed forces?

   __marine__ __naval__ __submarine__

8. Find a word that is related to *navigate*. __naval__

   Write another word from the same family. __navigation/navigator__

Vocabulary Power

Name _____

ANALOGIES

▶ In each half of an analogy, the words in the pair are related in the same way. Think about the relationships in the following pairs of words. Then complete the analogy. *Responses will vary.*

1. *Naval* is to *navy* as _____ is to *coast*.

2. *Fish* are to *gills* as _____ are to *lungs*.

3. *Oceanic* is to *marine* as *damp* is to _____.

4. A *ship* is to *nautical* as a _____ is to *agricultural*.

5. *Lobsters* are to *maritime* as _____ are to *arctic*.

6. A *mariner* is to a *sailor* as a _____ is to an *instructor*.

7. *Marine* is to an *adjective* as _____ is to a *noun*.

8. *Atlantic* is to *Maine* as _____ is to *California*.

9. *Arctic* is to *Ocean* as _____ is to *Sea*.

10. A *submarine* is to a *ship* as an *earthworm* is to a _____.

▶ Now try this. Choose two words from the box and think about their relationship to each other. Make an analogy by writing two words of your own that are related in the same way. The first one has been started for you. *Responses will vary.*

| ship | sail | sailor | waves |
| captain | anchor | dock | tides |

11. __Captain__ is to __sailor__ as _____ is to _____.

12. _____ is to _____ as _____ is to _____.

13. _____ is to _____ as _____ is to _____.

32 Unit 2 • Chapter 11   Vocabulary Power

CONTENT-AREA WORDS

A word map can show how words are related to each other. Read the following boxed words. Then look at the word map. Add words from the box to the word map by writing each word near the word it is most closely related to. One has been done for you.

fish	gulf	dunes	sharks	Atlantic	minerals
lobsters	oil	Pacific	bay	Indian	beach
Arctic	penguins	whales	oysters	seaweed	gas

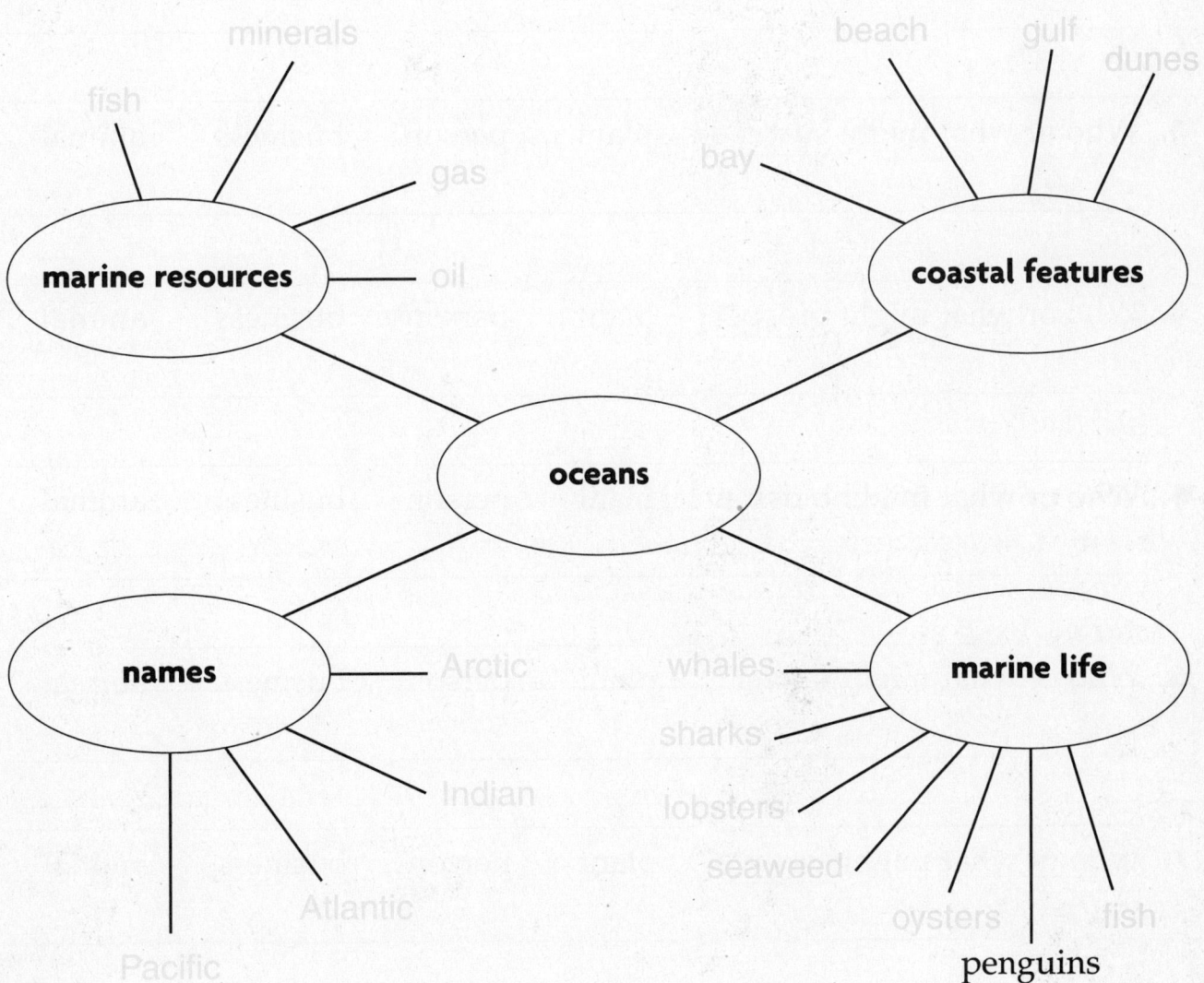

Vocabulary Power   Unit 2 • Chapter 11   33

Name _____

EXPLORE WORD MEANINGS

Answer the questions by circling all the words on the right that answer the questions. Write a sentence using the underlined word and one of the circled words. Sentences will vary. Accept reasonable responses.

1. Who or what might <u>thrive</u>? (plant) (person) (business) (animal)

_____

2. Who or what might <u>flourish</u>? (plant) (person) (business) animal

_____

3. Who or what might <u>succeed</u>? plant (person) (business) animal

_____

4. Who or what might <u>prosper</u>? plant (person) (business) animal

_____

5. Who or what might <u>blossom</u>? (plant) (person) business animal

_____

6. Who or what might <u>flower</u>? (plant) person business animal

_____

7. Who or what might <u>survive</u>? (plant) (person) (business) (animal)

_____

8. Who or what might <u>progress</u>? plant (person) (business) animal

_____

34 Unit 2 • Chapter 12   Vocabulary Power

Name _____

HOMOPHONES AND HOMOGRAPHS

▶ Homophones are words that sound the same but are spelled differently. Write the correct spelling of the word next to its definition.

1. flour   flower

   A rose or tulip _____flower_____

   B powdery substance made from wheat _____flour_____

2. hour   our

   A sixty minutes _____hour_____

   B belonging to us _____our_____

3. heal   he'll   heel

   A he will _____he'll_____

   B back of foot _____heel_____

   C make well _____heal_____

▶ Homographs are words that are spelled the same but are pronounced differently and have a different meaning. Write the pronunciation that matches the definition.

4. pro′gress   pro•gress′

   A to move forward _____pro•gress′_____

   B gradual improvement _____pro′gress_____

5. re′cord   re•cord′

   A document of past events _____re′cord_____

   B to set down in writing _____re•cord′_____

6. min′ute   mi•nute′

   A sixty seconds _____min′ute_____

   B very small _____mi•nute′_____

Vocabulary Power

Name _____

CONNOTATION/DENOTATION

▶ Rank the following groups of words.

1. From least to most healthy: thrive, succeed, blossom, survive

   __survive__ __succeed__ __blossom__ __thrive__

2. From fastest to slowest: jog, sprint, run, dash

   __jog__ __run__ __dash__ __sprint__

3. From least to most noticeable: speck, blotch, spot, smudge

   __speck__ __spot__ __smudge__ __blotch__

▶ The following pairs have similar meanings. Circle the word which has a more positive connotation. Explain your choice. Responses will vary.

4. (flourish)   flower _____

5. (prosper)   succeed _____

6. scheme   (plan) _____

7. spied   (watched) _____

36   Unit 2 • Chapter 12   Vocabulary Power

Name _____

CONTENT-AREA WORDS

Read the words in the box. Write each word where it belongs in the Venn diagram. Some words may fit in more than one category. Add words of your own to each category. Additional words will vary. Accept reasonable responses.

| subject | easel | landscape | acrylic |
| canvas | bristle | impression | palette |

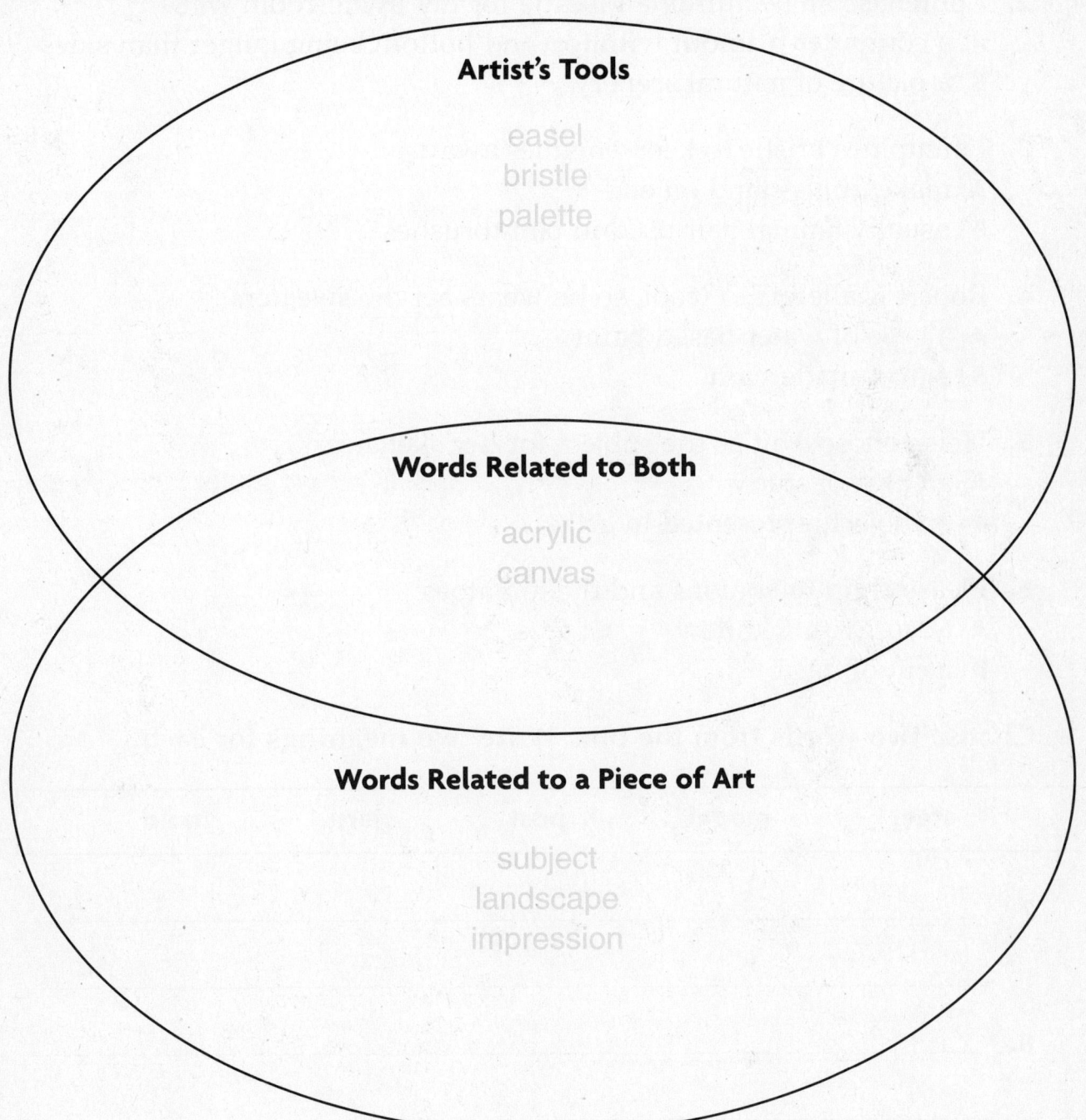

Vocabulary Power · Unit 3 • Chapter 13 · 37

Name _____

MULTIPLE-MEANING WORDS

▶ Read each sentence. Circle the letter for the definition that matches the underlined word.

1. The museum bought a canvas by Vincent van Gogh.
   (A) a painting, often done with oil paints
   B a heavy, coarse material

2. I purchased a beautiful landscape for my living-room wall.
   A a computer printout with top and bottom being longer than sides
   (B) a picture of natural scenery

3. Porcupines bristle to keep enemies away.
   (A) make quills stand on end
   B usually animal hair used in paintbrushes

4. Robert is allergic to wool, so he wears acrylic sweaters.
   A a type of water-based paint
   (B) a man-made yarn

5. Helen chose fruit as the subject for her sketches.
   A an area of study
   (B) an object represented in art

6. Please chop the onions and the tomatoes.
   (A) to cut with a knife
   B a cut of meat

▶ Choose two words from the box. Write two meanings for each.

| steer | model | post | yarn | mold |

7. _____

_____

8. _____

_____

38 Unit 3 • Chapter 13   Vocabulary Power

Name _____

ANALOGIES

▶ Each pair of words in an analogy is related in the same way. Complete the following analogies. Responses will vary. Accept reasonable responses.

1. An *easel* is to an *artist* as a *camera* is to a _____.

2. An *impression* is to _____ as an *image* is to *seeing*.

3. *Paint* is to *palette* as *film* is to _____.

4. A *meadow* is to a *landscape* as a _____ is to a *portrait*.

5. *Canvas* is to *fabric* as _____ is to *vehicle*.

6. *Bristle* is to *whistle* as _____ is to *wink*.

7. *Pale* is to *vibrant* as _____ is to *wild*.

8. *Texture* is to *bumpy* as *sound* is to _____.

9. A *sculptor* is to a *sculpture* as a _____ is to a *cake*.

10. *Artistic* is to *art* as _____ is to *music*.

11. *Show* is to *hide* as *tall* is to _____.

12. *Knead* is to _____ as *carve* is to *wood*.

▶ Now try this. Create the second half of the analogy by choosing two words that are related in the same way as the first pair of words.

13. A *zebra* is to a *horse* as a(n) _____ is to a(n) _____.

14. *Canada* is to *North America* as _____ is to _____.

15. *Colorful* is to *drab* as _____ is to _____.

16. _____ is to _____ as *hurry* is to *worry*.

Vocabulary Power   Unit 3 • Chapter 13   39

Name _____

EXPLORE WORD MEANINGS

▶ Read the words in the box. Then use them to answer the questions.

| fable | fiction | literature | poetry |
| myth | nonfiction | narrative | folktale |

1. Which one word is a label for all the others? _____literature_____

Now write the word that is a label for the following features.

2. has animals who behave like humans; teaches a lesson
   _____fable_____

3. true stories or facts about real life; purpose may be to inform
   _____nonfiction_____

4. a story that was first told orally; is passed down and often retold in slightly different ways _____folktale_____

5. did not really happen, but may seem realistic; may be fantasy; usually for entertainment _____fiction_____

6. may have rhythm and rhyme; uses figurative language to create images _____poetry_____

7. uses story structure; may be about an actual event
   _____narrative_____

8. fictional story from long ago; tries to explain why things are the way they are _____myth_____

▶ Now try this. Write the title of a piece of literature and choose the word from the box above that labels it.

Title _____

Genre or Label _____

Name _____

ANALOGIES

An analogy is made up of two pairs of words. Each pair of words is related in the same way. For example: *"Hot* is to *cold* as *tall* is to *short."*

▶ Look at each pair of words below. Decide how the words are related. Then complete the analogy. Accept reasonable responses.

1. *Literature* is to _____ as *dance* is to *ballet.*

2. *Award* is to *prize* as *little* is to _____.

3. *Folktale* is to *storyteller* as *song* is to _____.

4. *Author* is to *writer* as *eat* is to _____.

5. *Poetry* is to *poet* as _____ is to *playwright.*

6. *Diary* is to *journal* as *candy* is to _____.

7. *Fable* is to *instructional* as _____ is to *entertaining.*

8. *Narrative* is to *story* as *giggle* is to _____.

9. *Famous* is to *unknown* as *rough* is to _____.

10. *Myth* is to *fantasy* as _____ is to *reality.*

▶ Now try this. Think about the relationship between the two words provided. Then add another pair of words to complete the analogy. Accept reasonable responses.

11. *Keyboard* is to *pencil* as _____ is to _____.

12. *Leave* is to *stay* as _____ is to _____.

13. *Spring* is to *season* as _____ is to _____.

14. _____ is to _____ as *kitten* is to *cat.*

Vocabulary Power   Unit 3 • Chapter 14   41

Name _____

ANTONYMS

An antonym of a word can be formed by adding a prefix.

> un- and non- mean "not"

▶ Add a prefix to each of the words below to form its antonym.

1. __non__ + fiction = __nonfiction__

2. __un__ + realistic = __unrealistic__

3. __un__ + natural = __unnatural__

4. __non__ + flammable = __nonflammable__

▶ For each of the following word pairs, draw pictures to illustrate the differences between the antonyms. For example, draw the covers and create titles for a fiction and a nonfiction book.

5. fiction nonfiction	6. noisy quiet
7. addition subtraction	**8.** alone together

Name _____

SYNONYMS

▶ Match the words in the box with their synonyms.

| opportunity | serendipity | circumstance |
| occurrence | chance | probability |

1. likelihood _____probability_____

2. chance _____opportunity_____

3. incident _____occurrence_____

4. good fortune _____serendipity_____

5. situation _____circumstance_____

6. luck _____chance_____

▶ Replace the underlined words with a synonym from the box.

| chance | happenstance | airplane |
| occasion | probability | auditorium |

7. It was <u>chance</u> that led me to a career in music.
   _____happenstance_____

8. Mark took advantage of the <u>opportunity</u> to travel to Alaska.
   _____chance_____

9. The town's one-hundredth anniversary was an important <u>event</u>.
   _____occasion_____

10. There was a lot of excitement as the <u>hall</u> filled with guests.
    _____auditorium_____

11. The mayor had been out of town. He returned home in <u>a jet</u>.
    _____an airplane_____

12. The <u>likelihood</u> of rain was very slight, so the opening ceremony was held outdoors. _____probability_____

Vocabulary Power   Unit 3 • Chapter 15   43

Name _____

CLASSIFY/CATEGORIZE

In each group below, one word does not belong to the same category as the others. Circle the letter of that word. Then classify the remaining words by writing a label for that group.

1. A serendipity
   B happenstance
   C fortune
   (D) calamity

   related to having something
   good happen

2. F occasion
   G occurrence
   (H) mystery
   J event

   synonyms

3. A opportunity
   B occasion
   C chance
   (D) advertisement

   synonyms

4. (F) forecast
   G stormy
   H overcast
   J cloudless

   weather conditions

5. A snow
   B icicles
   C sleet
   (D) hurricane

   winter conditions

6. F hill
   (G) patio
   H mountain
   J slope

   land formations

7. A sergeant
   B corporal
   (C) sailor
   D captain

   military ranks

8. F ice cream
   G milk
   H cheese
   (J) bread

   dairy products

44 Unit 3 • Chapter 15   Vocabulary Power

Name _____

WORDS IN CONTEXT

| chance | circumstance | probability |
| opportunity | occurrence | |

Fill in the blanks to complete the weather forecast. Use each word only once.

1. Today there is a 90 percent _____chance_____ of rain, so take your raincoats and umbrellas!
2. Don't expect it to clear up before the weekend. The _____probability_____ of its continuing to rain is high.
3. Under these _____circumstance_____s, flooding is likely in low-lying areas.
4. This is a strange _____occurrence_____ for this time of year, which, as you know, is usually dry.
5. By next week, the rains should stop, and your gardens will have an _____opportunity_____ to dry out a bit.

DICTIONARY

Read the paragraph. Use the underlined words to add labels to the example of a dictionary page. Use the information in the paragraph to figure out where to place each label.

The two words at the top of a dictionary page are called <u>guide words</u>. These are the first and last words on the page. Each <u>entry word</u> is listed in dark type. Following each entry word is a <u>phonetic respelling</u> of the word. This shows how to pronounce or say the word. Next is the <u>part of speech</u>. This is often abbreviated. Finally, the <u>definition</u> of the word is given.

guide words — *entry word*

opportunity — orange

op•por•tu•ni•ty [op•ər•t(y)o͞o′nə•tē] *n.* A right or convenient time, occasion, or circumstance

phonetic respelling — *part of speech* — *definition*

Vocabulary Power Unit 3 • Chapter 15 45

Name _____

CLASSIFY/CATEGORIZE

In each group below, three words are related and one is not. Determine what category the words belong to, and then circle the letter of the word that does not belong. Add another word that fits the category.

1. A choreographer
   B conductor
   (C) program
   D usher

   Category: _____theatrical job titles_____

   Add: _____actor_____

2. F compose
   G orchestrate
   H perform
   (J) performance

   Category: _____musical action verbs_____

   Add: _____sing_____

3. A entertain
   (B) audience
   C please
   D delight

   Category: _____synonyms_____

   Add: _____amuse_____

4. F choreograph
   (G) chorus
   H telegraph
   J graphite

   Category: _____words with *graph*_____

   Add: _____photograph_____

5. A conduct
   B orchestra
   (C) tutu
   D cello

   Category: _____music words_____

   Add: _____(any musical instrument)_____

6. F scarf
   G boots
   H mittens
   (J) sandals

   Category: _____winter clothing_____

   Add: _____coat/jacket/gloves/hat_____

7. (A) cycling
   B tennis
   C baseball
   D football

   Category: _____sports played with a ball_____

   Add: _____(any ball sport)_____

8. F peach
   (G) potato
   H strawberry
   J pineapple

   Category: _____fruit_____

   Add: _____(any fruit)_____

46 Unit 3 • Chapter 16   Vocabulary Power

Name _____

SUFFIXES

The suffixes *-er, -or,* and *-ist* added to a verb change the meaning to "one who." Read below and follow the directions.

"City Performing Arts" is planning a grand performance for the opening of its downtown theatre.

▶ Give a title to the person or people who will do the following:

   1. <u>choreograph</u> the dance number _____

   2. <u>conduct</u> the orchestra _____
   3. <u>compose</u> original music for the opening act

   _____

   4. <u>perform</u> in the dance or drama acts _____

▶ Think of other people who might be needed. Write the verb that tells what he or she does and add a suffix. Remember that the audience does not see all the people involved in making the performance a success.

   For example: <u>drum</u> + <u>er</u> = <u>drummer</u>

   5. _____ + _____ = _____
   6. _____ + _____ = _____
   7. _____ + _____ = _____
   8. _____ + _____ = _____

▶ 9. What is the word meaning "one who entertains"? _____

   10. Can an *entertainer* be a *volunteer*? Why or why not? _____

   _____

   11. Can an *entertainer* be a *pioneer*? Why or why not? _____

   _____

Vocabulary Power

Name _____

COMPARE AND CONTRAST

▶ Think about the meanings of the underlined words in each question. Answer with complete sentences. Responses will vary.

1. Would you prefer to <u>entertain</u> or to be <u>entertained</u>? Why?

   _____

   _____

2. Which task is more complicated: to <u>orchestrate</u> or to <u>conduct</u>? Explain.

   _____

   _____

3. At a musical recital, would you prefer to be in the <u>audience</u> or be a <u>performer</u>? Explain. _____

   _____

   _____

▶ In each of the following pairs, compare and contrast the meanings of the words by noting how they are similar and how they are different. The first has been done for you.

4. performer, choreographer

   Compare: related to dancing or movement on stage

   Contrast: The choreographer does not perform in front of the audience.

5. composer, violinist

   Compare: related to music

   Contrast: The composer writes the music; the violinist plays it.

6. guitar, drum

   Compare: musical instruments

   Contrast: The guitar has strings.

Name _____

RELATED WORDS

The words in the box are all related to *carousel*. Look at the web below and decide which category each word fits. Write the words where they belong. Add some words of your own. Accept reasonable responses.

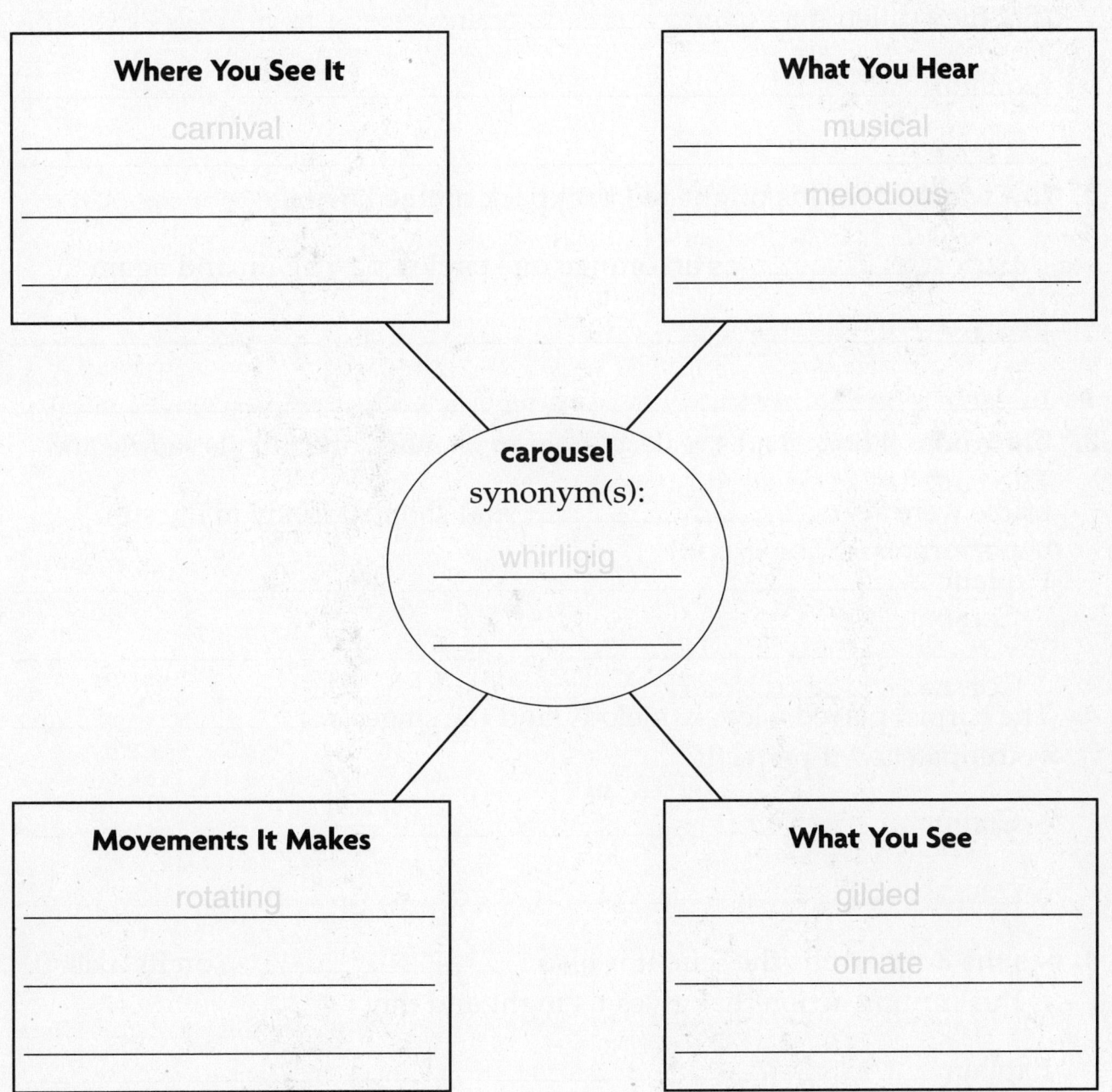

Vocabulary Power · Unit 3 • Chapter 17 · 49

Name _____

CONTEXT CLUES

Use context clues to complete the following sentences. Write a word from the box. Then explain how you chose that answer.

| carousel | whirligig | melodious | gilded | rotating |

1. The spinning top had a whirling motion. Grandpop says that in his day they called it a _____whirligig_____.

   Explain: __The word *whirligig* suggests a whirling motion.__ _____

2. Jim watched for his bright-red backpack on the baggage _____carousel_____ as an orange one circled past again and again.

   Explain: __The bag was passing again and again in a circular motion, just as a carousel does.__

3. The carousel horse had streaks of gold in its mane and tail. Its saddle and bridle were also _____gilded_____ and shone brightly in the sun.

   Explain: __The word *gilded* sounds something like *gold*, and gold shines.__

4. The harpist played a lovely melody, and the singer's _____melodious_____ voice matched it perfectly.

   Explain: __The word *melodious* is related to *melody*.__

5. As the Earth orbits the Sun, it is also _____rotating_____ on its axis. It is this turning action that gives us night and day.

   Explain: __*Rotating* means "turning."__

Name _____

COMPARE AND CONTRAST

▶ Fill in the chart below. In the first column, put an X in each box that correctly describes a carousel horse. In the second column, put an X in each box that describes a real horse.

	carousel horse	real horse
four legs	X	X
life size		X
smaller than life size	X	
stays in one place	X	
moves around freely		X
natural colors		X
painted colors	X	
mane	X	X
tail	X	X

Use the information from the chart to complete the lists below.

Similarities **Differences**

  Carousel Horse **Real Horse**

1. four legs   4. stays in one place   7. moves around freely

2. mane   5. painted colors   8. natural colors

3. tail   6. smaller than life size   9. life size

▶ Complete the following comparisons/contrasts.

10. *Musical* is like *noisy* except that _____

11. *Carnival* is like *celebration* because _____

12. *Ornate* is like *pretty* except that _____

Vocabulary Power   Unit 3 • Chapter 17   51

Name _____

RELATED WORDS

▶ Write words from the box to label the parts of the drawing below.

| pedestal | plaque | monument | dedication |

_____ monument

_____ pedestal

_____ dedication

_____ plaque

▶ Use the words in the box to complete the sentences. Then follow the directions in 2 and 3.

| podiatrist | scaffold | sculpt | pedestrian |

1. An artist hired to ____sculpt____ a statue is called a sculptor.
2. The statue needs to be restored. On the left side, draw a ____scaffold____ for the maintenance crew to climb onto.
3. The statue is in the town square. Draw a ____pedestrian____ walking by.
4. One of the work crew hurt his foot and has to go to a ____podiatrist____, or a foot specialist.

Name _____

GREEK AND LATIN ROOTS

Look at the Latin roots in the box below and their meanings. Knowing these common roots can sometimes help you figure out the meaning of an unfamiliar word.

Latin root Meaning	*cent* hundred	*tri* three	*quad* four	*-ian* one who
Greek root Meaning	*-iatry* art of healing	*ped* or *pod* foot	*meter* measure	

▶ Complete the *ped/pod* web below. Read the definitions and use the roots provided above to write the word described.

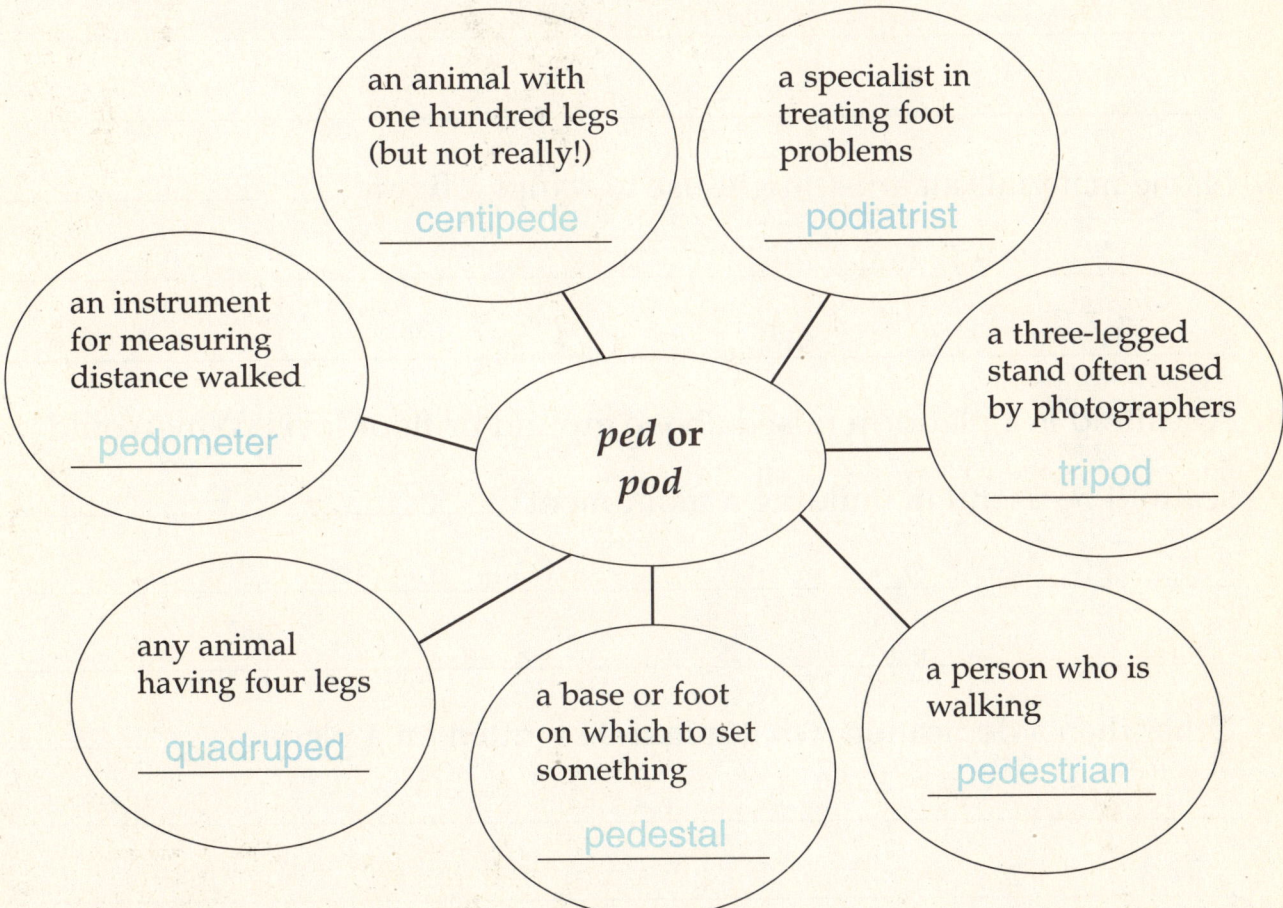

- an animal with one hundred legs (but not really!) — **centipede**
- a specialist in treating foot problems — **podiatrist**
- an instrument for measuring distance walked — **pedometer**
- a three-legged stand often used by photographers — **tripod**
- any animal having four legs — **quadruped**
- a base or foot on which to set something — **pedestal**
- a person who is walking — **pedestrian**

▶ Now list other words of your own that use any of the roots above.

Possible responses: pedal, podiatry, percent, century, triangle, quadrant, thermometer, musician

Vocabulary Power   Unit 3 • Chapter 18   53

Name _____

EXPLORE WORD MEANINGS

Think about the meaning of the underlined words. Then write your answer to each question.

1. Other than on a statue, where might you see a <u>dedication</u>? Possible responses: on a music CD; the first page of a book; the cornerstone of a public building

2. What purpose does a <u>monument</u> have? Possible response: A monument reminds people of someone great or something important.

   Who or what would you build a monument for? Explain your reasons. Responses will vary.

3. Name materials an artist might use to <u>sculpt</u> a figure. Possible responses: clay, papier-mâché, wood, stone

4. A <u>scaffold</u> is a platform raised above ground or floor level. Why would a scaffold be useful in building a monument? Possible response: A monument is often very large, and a ladder might not be tall enough.

5. Other than a dedication, what might be written on a <u>plaque</u>? Possible response: any kind of information for public viewing, such as facts about animals at a zoo, the history of a building, etc.

6. What would a <u>monumental</u> earthquake be like? Possible response: It would be a very strong earthquake that causes a lot of damage.

Name _____

EXPLORE WORD MEANINGS

▶ Write each of the words from the box under the categories below. Some words may fit in more than one category.

vapor	surroundings	climate	smog
ozone	atmosphere	ambiance	oxygen

Science words

_____

_____

_____

_____

_____

Weather words

_____

_____

_____

_____

_____

Describes the area around you

_____

_____

_____

_____

_____

Words with two syllables

_____

_____

_____

_____

_____

▶ Now answer these questions. Think about the meaning of the underlined words.

1. Would you prefer to breathe <u>oxygen</u> or <u>smog</u>? Explain why.

   _____

2. How is a restaurant's <u>ambiance</u> similar to its <u>surroundings</u>? How is it different? _____

   _____

Vocabulary Power   Unit 4 • Chapter 19   55

Name _____

MULTIPLE-MEANING WORDS

Determine the meaning of the underlined word as it is used in each sentence. Write the letter of the definition that matches each.

1. The smoke from vast forest fires added to the pollution of the atmosphere. __A__
   There was an atmosphere of sportsmanship when the opposing teams met for the first time. __B__
   A the layer of air surrounding the earth
   B the surrounding feeling of an environment

2. Citrus trees, such as the orange and tangerine, grow best in a tropical climate. __B__
   The townspeople couldn't get enough of Yulee's Yummy Yogurt. The climate was right for Yulee to open a second store. __A__
   A an atmosphere or feeling among people
   B a region having particular weather conditions

3. Ron felt homesick at first, but he soon felt comfortable in his new surroundings. __B__
   The trees surrounding the lake were tall and leafy, providing shade for campers. __A__
   A enclosing on all sides
   B the conditions around you

4. Jerome auditioned for the lead part in the musical. __A__
   Songbirds and crickets are among the musical animals that live in the woods. __B__
   A a dramatic performance that includes singing
   B melodious, sounding like music

56 Unit 4 • Chapter 19   Vocabulary Power

Name _____

CLASSIFY/CATEGORIZE

In each of the following groups, three of the words are related in some way. Circle the letter of the one word that is not part of the group. Then name the category and add another word that fits.

1. A stream
   B waterfall
   (C) glacier
   D brook

   Category: moving water

   Add: river, spring, ocean

2. A oxygen
   (B) hydroplane
   C hydrogen
   D ozone

   Category: gases

   Add: nitrogen, helium

3. A vapor
   (B) sand
   C fumes
   D gases

   Category: things you can't see or touch

   Add: air, wind

4. A ambiance
   B mood
   (C) joyfulness
   D atmosphere

   Category: synonyms

   Add: feeling, environment

5. A cozy
   (B) circle
   C uncomfortable
   D crowded

   Category: adjectives (that describe a place/room)

   Add: pleasant, warm, untidy

6. A atmosphere
   B spherical
   (C) sphinx
   D biosphere

   Category: word family, related to sphere

   Add: sphere, hemisphere

7. A fog
   B haze
   C cloud
   (D) warmth

   Category: things you see in the sky

   Add: stars, sun, moon

8. (A) jumping jacks
   B on foot
   C bus
   D bicycle

   Category: ways to get around

   Add: car, train

Vocabulary Power   Unit 4 • Chapter 19   57

Name _____

GREEK AND LATIN ROOTS

Many English words are borrowed from other languages. In Greek, the root *astro* means "star" or "star-shaped." Think about this information as you write answers for the following questions.

Possible responses are given.

1. *Nautical* comes from the Greek word for *sailor*. What does *astronaut* mean?

   someone who sails through the stars

2. The endings *-ics*, *-ogy*, and *-y* mean "the science or practice of." What does *astronautics* mean?

   the science of traveling in space

   What is *astronomy*?

   the study of the stars

3. The suffix *-er* often means "a person who." What does an *astronomer* do?

   studies the stars

4. If a *cuboid* is an object shaped something like a cube, what do you think an *asteroid* is?

   something that resembles a star

5. If *nautical* means "having to do with the sea," what do you think *astral* means?

   having to do with the stars

6. A dome is a rounded roof. What might an *astrodome* be used for?

   An astrodome might be a clear roof through which people might look at the stars.

7. An aster is a type of flower. Draw what you think it might look like.

8. An asterisk is a kind of punctuation mark. Draw what you think it might look like.

58 Unit 4 • Chapter 20   Vocabulary Power

Name _____

COMPARE AND CONTRAST

Complete the following statements. Responses will vary.

1. An *astronomer* is like a *geographer* except that _____
   _____

2. An *asterisk* is like a *question mark* because _____
   _____

3. An *aster* is like a *zinnia* because _____
   _____

4. *Binoculars* are like a *telescope* except that _____
   _____

5. *Mars* is like *Jupiter* except that _____
   _____

6. *Dusk* is like *dawn* because _____
   _____

7. *Sunshine* is like *moonlight* but _____
   _____

8. A *space shuttle* is like an *airplane* except that _____
   _____

9. *Stars* are like a *galaxy* except that _____
   _____

Vocabulary Power

Name _____

RELATED WORDS

Words can be related in several ways. They may have the same suffix or prefix, the same root word, or similar meanings. Circle the letter of the word that is NOT related to the others in each list. Then identify the category or relationship of the other words.

1. A astronaut
   B astrodome
   (C) astray
   D astronomer

   same root word

2. F astronomy
   G geology
   (H) story
   J chemistry

   sciences

3. A nautical
   (B) naughty
   C astronautics
   D aeronautics

   same root word

4. F astronomical
   G gigantic
   H enormous
   (J) size

   similar meanings

5. A energy
   B energize
   C energetic
   (D) enemy

   same root word

6. F rotation
   (G) rotten
   H rotating
   J rotary

   same root word

7. A aster
   B asterisk
   (C) astern
   D asteroid

   same root word

8. F vertical
   G horizontal
   H diagonal
   (J) astral

   directions

9. A gas
   B gases
   (C) gash
   D gaseous

   same root word

10. F sunrise
    G sunup
    (H) dusk
    J dawn

    similar meanings

60 Unit 4 • Chapter 20   Vocabulary Power

Name _____

RELATED WORDS

▶ Write each word from the box where it belongs.

auditory	nocturnal	perception	extra-sensitive
ocular	olfactory	diurnal	extraordinary

Labels for senses
auditory
ocular
olfactory

Labels for time
diurnal
nocturnal

Means "out of the ordinary"
extraordinary

Means "unusually sensitive"
extra-sensitive

Synonym for *sense*
perception

▶ Choose a word from the box above to complete each sentence.

1. *Audible* means "can be heard." The _____auditory_____ sense is related to the ears.

2. *Oculist* is a synonym for *optometrist*. The _____ocular_____ sense is related to the eyes.

3. *Olfaction* is the sense of smell. The _____olfactory_____ sense is related to the nose.

Vocabulary Power

Name _____

PREFIXES

▶ The prefix *extra-* comes from a Latin root that means "beyond" or "outside of." Use this information to complete the following.

1. extra = beyond or outside of   curricular = related to the curriculum

   extra + curricular = _____extracurricular_____

   What is an extracurricular activity? _Possible response: It is an activity a student takes part in that is not part of the curriculum._

   List some examples. _Examples will vary._

2. extra = beyond or outside of   mural = having to do with walls

   extra + mural = _____extramural_____

   What are extramural sports competitions? _Possible response: sports competitions that take place outside of the school grounds, with students from another school_

3. Complete the equation to form a word that means "beyond the ordinary."

   _____extra_____ + _____ordinary_____ = _____extraordinary_____

4. Mike's dad likes to cook chili, but his chili is hotter than the usual. He cooks with unusually hot peppers. His chili is outside of the ordinary. It is *extraordinarily* hot! That's not an easy word to say, so he just calls it extra-hot. Draw a picture of someone tasting extra-hot chili.

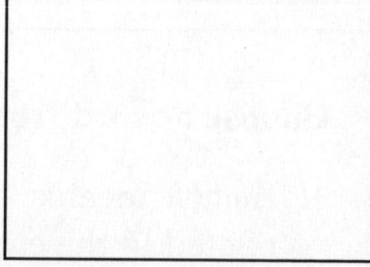

▶ *Extra* is a shortened form of *extraordinary*. With a hyphen, it can be used as a prefix to mean "unusually." In the sentences below, write your ideas.

5. Dogs have a good sense of smell. Extra-sensitive noses are good for _Possible response: tracking down lost people._

6. Extra-sensitive hearing means that bats are able to _Possible response: hunt their prey by listening to its movements in the dark._

Name _____

ANALOGIES

▶ The words in each half of an analogy are related in the same way. Determine the relationship between one pair of words. Then complete the analogy. Accept reasonable responses.

1. *Auditory* is to the *ear* as *ocular* is to the _____.

2. *Olfactory* is to *perfume* as _____ is to *wind chimes*.

3. An *owl* is to *nocturnal* as _____ is to *diurnal*.

4. *Perception* is to *perceive* as *reception* is to _____.

5. *Extraordinary* is to *commonplace* as *sprinting* is to _____.

6. A *bat* is to *wings* as a *fish* is to _____.

7. A *mane* is to a *horse* as *whiskers* are to _____.

8. A *nose* is to *sniff* as *eyes* are to _____.

9. *Fingers* are to *toes* as a *wrist* is to an _____.

10. An *eagle* is to *vision* as _____ is to *swiftness*.

11. *Glove* is to *hand* as _____ is to *foot*.

12. *Sharp* is to *dull* as *bright* is to _____.

▶ Now try this. The first half of the analogy is provided. Write a pair of words that is related in the same way.

13. An *alligator* is to a *reptile* as _____ is to _____.

14. *Seeing* is to *hearing* as _____ is to _____.

15. *Water* is to a *pond* as _____ is to _____.

16. *Bear* is to *cub* as _____ is to _____.

Vocabulary Power

Name _____

CONTEXT CLUES

Read each sentence, paying attention to the underlined word. On the line, write the word's meaning. Possible responses are given.

1. We went to the arboretum to see the rare trees and shrubs.

    Arboretum means _a place to study and observe rare trees_.

2. In botany class, we studied about plants.

    Botany means _the study of plants_.

3. The botanist carefully studies the leaves and roots of the plant.

    Botanist means _a scientist who studies plants_.

4. Oaks, pines, and many smaller plants make up the flora of our area.

    Flora means _the plants of a particular area_.

5. The warm greenhouse had a variety of delicate tropical plants.

    Greenhouse means _a heated building used for growing delicate plants_.

6. The farmer grew flowers and vegetables in her garden.

    Garden means _a plot of land for growing plants_.

7. The cows grazed in the lush valley, as there was little vegetation on the barren hillsides.

    Vegetation means _plant life_.

8. The botanical setting had many flowers and trees.

    Botanical means _having to do with plants_.

9. When the rosebushes bloom, they will produce beautiful red flowers.

    Bloom means _to produce flowers_.

Name _____

CLASSIFY/CATEGORIZE

Things that are alike in some way can be classified. The name of the category tells how the things are alike. Write each of the words from the box below under the correct heading. Then add three words of your own to each category. Accept reasonable responses.

foliage	flourish	arboretum
nature preserve	botanical garden	greenhouse
flora	prosper	roots
thrive	vegetation	blossom

Things a Botanist Studies	Places a Botanist Might Work	Words to Describe the Way Healthy Plants Grow
flora	greenhouse	flourish
vegetation	arboretum	prosper
foliage	botanical garden	thrive
roots	nature preserve	blossom

Vocabulary Power   Unit 4 • Chapter 22

Name _____

COMPARE AND CONTRAST

Complete the following statements.

Responses may vary. Possible responses are given.

1. *Botany* is like *biology* except that biology is the study of plants and animals while botany is only the study of plants.

2. A *garden* is like a *greenhouse* because they are both places to grow plants.

3. A *botanist* is like a *geologist* except that botanists study plants and geologists study rocks.

4. An *arboretum* is like a *forest* except that arboretums have rare trees and plants.

5. A *flower stem* is like a *tree trunk* because they both support the plant.

6. *Flora* is like *vegetation* because they are both plant life.

7. An *evergreen* is like a *deciduous tree* except that deciduous trees lose their leaves and evergreens don't.

8. An *aster* is like a *rose* because they are both flowers.

9. An *oak tree* is like a *pine tree* except that the oak has leaves and the pine has needles.

10. A *garden* is like a *farm* because they are both places to grow things.

66 Unit 4 • Chapter 22   Vocabulary Power

Name _____

CONTENT-AREA WORDS

Read the words in the box. Determine which category each word belongs in. Write the words in the web below. Then add your own words to each category. Additional words will vary. Accept reasonable responses.

barren	abrasion	wear	gravel
windswept	glacier	weathering	coastline

Synonyms
abrasion
wear
weathering

Causes
gravel
glacier

EROSION

Places Affected
coastline

Words That Describe
windswept
barren

Vocabulary Power — Unit 4 • Chapter 23

Name _____

ANALOGIES

An analogy makes a comparison. Think about the relationship between the words in the first pair. Circle the letter of the word that best completes each analogy.

1. *Wear* is to *erosion* as *cyclone* is to _____.
   A drizzle
   B blizzard
   C sunshine
   (D) tornado

2. *Sand* is to *dunes* as _____ are to *mountains*.
   F streams
   G clouds
   (H) rocks
   J trees

3. *Abrasion* is to *gravel* as *irrigation* is to _____.
   (A) water
   B soil
   C sand
   D clouds

4. *Furnace* is to *cold* as _____ is to *hot*.
   F slippers
   (G) glacier
   H bulb
   J sun

5. *Rain* is to *snow* as _____ is to *ice*.
   A cold
   B hard
   (C) water
   D clear

6. *Desert* is to *sandy* as *arctic* is to _____.
   (F) icy
   G far
   H sweltering
   J rainy

7. *Grains* are to _____ as *droplets* are to *rain*.
   A boulders
   B shells
   C grass
   (D) sand

8. *Blew* is to the *wind* as _____ is to a *volcano*.
   F fell
   (G) erupted
   H clapped
   J struck

Name _____

SYNONYMS AND ANTONYMS

▶ Words with nearly the same meaning are called *synonyms*. Replace each underlined word with a synonym from the word box. Write the new sentences.

| weathering | coastline | inquired | simple |

1. We <u>asked</u> about the cause of the landslide.
   We inquired about the cause of the landslide.
2. Huge waves pounded the <u>shore</u>.
   Huge waves pounded the coastline.
3. Science is an <u>easy</u> subject for me.
   Science is a simple subject for me.
4. The old cabin showed signs of <u>wear</u>.
   The old cabin showed signs of weathering.

▶ Words that have opposite meanings are called *antonyms*. Replace each underlined word with an *antonym* from the word box to change the meaning of the sentence. Write the new sentences.

| erosion | windswept | difficult | refused |

5. Harsh winds had resulted in <u>conservation</u> of the soil.
   Harsh winds had resulted in erosion of the soil.
6. We climbed a steep and <u>sheltered</u> cliff.
   We climbed a steep and windswept cliff.
7. I struggled to answer the <u>easy</u> question.
   I struggled to answer the difficult question.
8. My mom <u>agreed</u> to give me dessert before dinner.
   My mom refused to give me dessert before dinner.

Vocabulary Power

Name _____

SYNONYMS

▶ *Devastate* was used in each sentence below, but it is not the best word. Choose the synonym from the box that best fits the meaning of the sentence.

harm	spoil	destroy	obliterate

1. The dog will not <u>devastate</u> you.
   Possible response: harm

2. A tornado can <u>devastate</u> houses.
   Possible response: destroy

3. A raging fire can completely <u>devastate</u> a forest, leaving only ashes.
   Possible response: obliterate

4. Too much salt will <u>devastate</u> the taste of the soup.
   Possible response: spoil

▶ Replace *rebuild* with a better synonym from the box.

refurbish	renovate	restore	revive

5. We will <u>rebuild</u> the old house, making it look new.
   Possible response: renovate

6. We will clean the painting to <u>rebuild</u> it to its original beauty.
   Possible response: restore

7. A mug of hot chocolate will <u>rebuild</u> the cold, tired children.
   Possible response: revive

8. We will add some new curtains and a coat of paint to <u>rebuild</u> the room.
   Possible response: refurbish

Name _____

WORD FAMILIES

Word families are made up of words that have the same root or base word. Read the words below. Circle the letter of the word that does not belong. Then replace it with a word of your own. Additional words may vary. Possible responses are given.

1. A demolish
   B demolition
   C demolishing
   (D) detract

   demolished

2. (F) dessert
   G destroy
   H destroyer
   J destroys

   destroyed

3. A devastate
   (B) vest
   C devastation
   D devastated

   devastating

4. F obliterate
   G obliteration
   (H) object
   J obliterating

   obliterated

5. A refurbish
   B refurbishes
   (C) furniture
   D refurbished

   refurbishing

6. F renovate
   (G) renown
   H renovation
   J renovated

   renovating

7. (A) resistance
   B restoration
   C restore
   D restored

   restoring

8. F revive
   G revived
   H revives
   (J) revisit

   reviving

Vocabulary Power — Unit 4 • Chapter 24

Name _____

EXPLORE WORD MEANINGS

Read and respond to each question or statement.

Responses will vary. Possible responses are given.

1. How would you **revive** a plant that is drooping? give it water, give it fertilizer, move it to a sunny window

   ┌─ Draw pictures of the plant before and after it was revived. ─┐
   │ Students may use a separate sheet of paper for drawings.   │
   │   │
   │ Before   After   │
   └──┘

2. What things might you do to **refurbish** your bedroom? clean it, repaint it, get new curtains, get a new comforter or bedspread, put up posters

   ┌─ Draw pictures of your bedroom before and after it is refurbished. ─┐
   │   │
   │ Before   After   │
   └──┘

3. If a storm were to devastate a community, what are some things that would need to be done to **restore** it? rebuild houses, rebuild businesses, clean up streets and neighborhoods

   ┌─ Draw pictures of the community before and after it was restored. ─┐
   │   │
   │ Before   After   │
   └───┘

Name _____

COMPARE AND CONTRAST

▶ Describe urban and rural communities by checking each box that applies. Remember that rural areas also have small towns.

	boulevard	lane	skyscraper	ranch	downtown	city center	subway	civic	municipal	metropolitan	agriculture	commerce
Urban	X		X		X	X	X	X	X	X		X
Rural		X		X	X			X	X		X	X

▶ Make a list showing how an urban community is like a rural community. Make two lists showing their differences. Use the information from the chart.

Likenesses

downtown

municipal

commerce

civic

Differences

Urban	**Rural**
boulevard	lane
skyscraper	ranch
city center	agriculture
subway	
metropolitan	

Vocabulary Power

Name _____

COMPOUND WORDS

Compound words are made up of two words. The two words may be joined together, hyphenated, or kept separate.

    For example: armchair   old-fashioned   ice cream

▶ Form two more compound words using part of the first word given.

1. armchair   arm _rest_____   arm _wrestle_____

2. downtown   _up_____ town   _mid_____ town

    down _river_____   down _hill_____

3. skyscraper   sky _diver_____   sky _light_____

4. watercolor   water _cooler_____   water _fall_____

COINED WORDS

Before the first skyscraper was built, the word *skyscraper* did not exist. The word was coined, or invented, because a name was needed for this new type of building. As new ideas or inventions appear, people need to create new words. For example, most of the words related to computers are new words.

▶ Read the descriptions below and write the word from the box that matches each.

| webmaster | pixel | byte | Internet |

1. a unit of data _byte_____
2. the person in charge of creating and maintaining a website

    _webmaster_____

3. one spot out of thousands on a computer screen, out of which pictures are formed _pixel_____

4. an international collection of computer networks _Internet_____

Name _____

CONNOTATION/DENOTATION

▶ Rank the following groups of words in the correct order.

1. From shortest to tallest: house, skyscraper, tent, apartment building

   tent _____ house _____ apartment building _____ skyscraper

2. From smallest to greatest: civic, municipal, federal, state

   municipal _____ civic _____ state _____ federal

3. From most passengers to fewest passengers: bicycle, subway, car, bus

   subway _____ bus _____ car _____ bicycle

4. From narrowest to widest: boulevard, highway, footpath, avenue

   footpath _____ avenue _____ boulevard _____ highway

▶ Think about the meaning of the underlined words. Then answer each question, giving reasons for your answer. Responses will vary. Accept reasonable responses.

5. Would you prefer to live in an urban area or a metropolitan area? Why? _____

_____

6. Would you prefer to own a skyscraper or a highrise? Why?

_____

7. Would you prefer to walk along a road or a boulevard? Why?

_____

Vocabulary Power   Unit 5 • Chapter 25   75

Name _____

EXPLORE WORD MEANINGS

▶ Write the word(s) from the box that best answer the questions that follow.

| heritage | legacy | inheritance | ancestor |
| history | heredity | genealogy | origin |

1. What word names a relative who lived long ago?
   __ancestor__

2. Which three words are related to the Latin root *heres*, which means "heir"? __heritage__ __heredity__
   __inheritance__

3. Which word means "the study of one's family history"?
   __genealogy__

4. This word means "the place where something began."
   __origin__

5. Which word means "the study of the past"? __history__

6. Which words mean "something handed down from previous generations"? __heritage__ __legacy__

7. Which word means the opposite of *descendant*?
   __ancestor__

▶ Synonyms sometimes have slightly different denotations. Write the word that best fits the definition below.

genealogy   history

  A includes stories about what people were like and what they did
    __history__

  B a record of names, dates, and places of birth, marriage, and death
    __genealogy__

76 Unit 5 • Chapter 26   Vocabulary Power

Name _____

CONTEXT CLUES

Read each sentence and think about the meaning of the underlined word. Write a definition for the word as it is used in the sentence.

Possible responses are given.

1. The origin of Trina's family name was uncertain, but it seemed to be Scandinavian.

   Origin means _the place where something comes from_____.

2. Bradley is proud of his Scottish heritage, and is learning to play the bagpipes.

   Heritage means _the customs, traditions, and culture of a family_____.

3. One of Shawna's ancestors fought in the American Civil War.

   Ancestors means _family members who lived a long time ago_____.

4. My grandmother is researching her genealogy. She wants to find the first American in the family.

   Genealogy means _a person's line of descent_____.

5. Black hair and green eyes are part of my heredity from my father's side of the family.

   Heredity means _the physical characteristics passed down through a family_____.

6. This antique nightstand is my mother's inheritance from her grandmother.

   Inheritance means _an item of some value handed down by a relative_____.

Vocabulary Power   Unit 5 • Chapter 26   77

Name _____

CLASSIFY/CATEGORIZE

▶ In each list of words below, three words belong to the same category and one does not. Circle the letter of the word that does not belong. Name the category for the other words, and then add another word that fits.

1. A legacy
   B heritage
   C inheritance
   (D) descendants

   Category: handed down from the past

   Add: customs, heredity

2. (F) skating
   G mathematics
   H science
   J history

   Category: school subjects

   Add: art, reading, etc.

3. A genealogy
   B cardiology
   (C) geography
   D biology

   Category: words ending in -logy

   Add: geology

4. F language
   G physical traits
   H customs
   (J) fruit trees

   Category: related to heritage

   Add: traditions, history

5. A photographs
   (B) trains
   C birth certificates
   D letters

   Category: personal history

   Add: marriage certificates

6. F Native American
   G Egyptian
   (H) Canada
   J Korean

   Category: nationalities

   Add: Canadian, etc.

▶ Now try this. Create your own categories, and list three items that fit.

7. A _____
   B _____
   C _____

   Category: _____

8. A _____
   B _____
   C _____

   Category: _____

78 Unit 5 • Chapter 26   Vocabulary Power

Name _____

CONTEXT CLUES

Read the following story. Use context clues to help you choose the correct word from the box. Fill in the blanks, using each word only once.

| transatlantic | transcontinental | translate | transparent |
| transmountain | transoceanic | transport | translucent |

    Josh and Henry decided to travel around the world and visit many countries. They started their world tour in West Africa. They traveled by ship across the Atlantic Ocean. The _____transatlantic_____ journey took two weeks. The cabin they stayed in had a _____translucent_____ window, so although it let sunlight into the room, they could not see the outside.

    They docked in New York City, and soon after began their travels across the North American continent. Eventually, they reached San Francisco, on the west coast. Their _____transcontinental_____ journey was long but a lot of fun.

    They had especially enjoyed their _____transmountain_____ hike across the Rocky Mountains. Once, they stopped at a mountain spring with crystal-clear water. They had never seen such a _____transparent_____ pool. Josh had wanted to _____transport_____ some of the water back home, but they still had far to go.

    From California, the men needed to cross the ocean once again, to get to Japan. This time they decided to fly. The _____transoceanic_____ journey was much faster by plane than by ship! In Japan, they needed someone to _____translate_____ for them in the restaurant. They were very glad to find a waiter who spoke English!

Vocabulary Power   Unit 5 • Chapter 27

Name _____

EXPLORE WORD MEANINGS

Read and answer each question. Think about the meaning of the underlined word.

1. You are going on a <u>transatlantic</u> journey. What type of transportation would you prefer and why?

   _____

   _____

   Where would your journey begin and where would it end?

   _____

2. You are going on a <u>transcontinental</u> journey. What continent will you travel through? Name some sights you hope to see there.

   _____

   _____

3. What does <u>transpacific</u> mean?

   _____

4. What would be a good way to <u>transport</u> a case of lightbulbs?

   _____

   _____

5. How might one make a <u>transmountain</u> trip?

   _____

   _____

6. Would you prefer the windows in your home to be <u>transparent</u> or <u>translucent</u>? Explain your reasons.

   _____

   _____

Name _____

WORD FAMILIES

Words that share the same root, base word, prefix, or suffix belong to a word family. Read the word families below. Write the root, base word, prefix, or suffix for each family.

1. transcontinental, continentalism, continental _____ continent _____
2. economist, economics, economically _____ economy _____
3. settlement, resettlement, settler _____ settle _____
4. transoceanic, oceanography, oceanfront _____ ocean _____
5. informational, informatively, informant _____ inform _____
6. marina, mariner, aquamarine _____ marine _____
7. explainable, explanation, explanatory _____ explain _____
8. glaciology, glacial, glaciation _____ glacier _____
9. analyst, analytics, analysis _____ analyze _____
10. geologist, geological, geologize _____ geology _____
11. mountainous, transmountain, mountaineer _____ mountain _____
12. strategize, strategist, strategic _____ strategy _____
13. transparent, translate, translucent _____ trans _____
14. sequential, sequentially, sequencing _____ sequence _____
15. relative, relationship, relatedness _____ relate _____
16. transport, deportation, import _____ port _____
17. urbane, urbanite, suburban _____ urban _____
18. disinterested, interestingly, uninteresting _____ interest _____

Vocabulary Power   Unit 5 • Chapter 27   81

Name _____

RELATED WORDS

Use the words from the box to answer the questions that follow.

| irrigate | trough | canal | moisten |
| aqueduct | hydrate | sluice | drench |

1. Four words that are synonyms for "to water."

   _____irrigate_____   _____moisten_____

   _____hydrate_____   _____drench_____

2. Which would you do regularly, as on a farm? ___irrigate___

3. Which would you do if the soil were just slightly dry? __moisten or hydrate__

4. Which would you need to do if the soil were extremely dry?

   _____drench_____

5. Four words that are ways to hold or carry water.

   _____trough_____   _____canal_____

   _____aqueduct_____   _____sluice_____

6. Which one has a gate to control the flow of the water? ___sluice___

7. Which one can be small enough to bring water to fields, or large enough for ships to sail on? ___canal___

8. Write your own words related to water. Accept reasonable responses.

   _____   _____   _____

   _____   _____   _____

   _____   _____   _____

82 Unit 5 • Chapter 28   Vocabulary Power

Name _____

WORD FAMILIES

▶ Words related by a root or base word belong to the same family. Circle the letter of the word that is not related to the others in the list.

1. A irrigate
   B irrigation
   C irrigating
   (D) irritate

2. F moisten
   G moisturize
   H moist
   (J) mostly

3. (A) hybrid
   B hydrate
   C dehydrated
   D hydrant

4. F aqueduct
   G aquifer
   (H) acquire
   J aquarium

▶ Words can also be related by structural elements such as prefixes, suffixes, or word parts. Circle the letter of the word that is not related to the others in the list. Then add your own to the list. *Possible responses are given.*

5. (A) runner
   B jumping
   C throwing
   D playing

   Add: _running_

6. F independent
   G incorrect
   (H) island
   J indirect

   Add: _inedible_

7. A regularly
   B rapidly
   (C) energy
   D frequently

   Add: _joyfully_

8. F redo
   (G) reach
   H rerun
   J reheat

   Add: _retell_

9. (A) ouch
   B out-yell
   C outwalk
   D outswim

   Add: _outdo_

10. F fields
    G tigers
    H mittens
    (J) mint

    Add: _mints_

Vocabulary Power

Unit 5 • Chapter 28   83

Name _____

CONTEXT CLUES

Context clues can help you determine the meaning of an unfamiliar word. Read the following sentences. Write a definition for the underlined word. Look for clues in the other words in the sentence.

1. In dry parts of the country, farmers use irrigation to bring water to their crops. _____Possible response: a system of watering crops_____

2. A canal was built, leading from the lake to the farthest field, to bring water to the crops.
_____Possible response: a man-made waterway for irrigation_____

3. Farmers must be very knowledgeable about the climate, or weather conditions, in their area.
_____Possible response: the weather in an area_____

4. We needed a heavy rain to drench the vegetable garden before it dried out completely.
_____Possible response: wet thoroughly_____

5. When the apples are ripe, farmers harvest them and take them to market.
_____Possible response: to gather a crop_____

6. If you want to raise crops and farm animals, you should study agriculture in college.
_____Possible response: the science of raising crops and farm animals_____

7. As the stream had dried up, we kept a trough filled with water for the cows to drink.
_____Possible response: a container for animals to drink from_____

8. When there is enough water in the canal, the sluice is closed.
_____Possible response: a gate through which water passes_____

Name _____

RELATED WORDS

Around the web are definitions of words related to rivers. Fill in each blank with a word from the box that matches the definition.

delta	inlet	meander	valley
oasis	tidal	tributary	source

__valley__
a low point between hills or mountains

__tributary__
a stream that feeds into a larger stream or river

__source__
the beginning point

__meander__
to follow a winding course

river

__oasis__
a fertile area in a desert, often along a riverbank

__delta__
the flat area of land at the mouth of a river

__inlet__
a narrow strip of water leading into land from the ocean

__tidal__
having to do with the ocean tides

Vocabulary Power

Name _____

COMPARE AND CONTRAST

Complete the following sentences to describe how the two items in italics are alike or how they are different. The first has been done for you.

1. A *delta* is like a *plain* because they are both flat and they both support crops.

2. A *river* is like a *stream* except that _Accept reasonable responses._____ .

3. To *meander* is like *to flow* but _____ .

4. A *tributary* is like a *branch* because _____ .

5. A *water fountain* is like an *oasis* because _____ .

6. A *canyon* is like a *valley* but _____ .

7. An *inlet* is like a *harbor* except that _____ .

8. A *snow flurry* is like a *drizzle* because _____ .

9. A *tidal pool* is like a *pond* except that _____ .

86 Unit 5 • Chapter 29   Vocabulary Power

Name _____

ANALOGIES

▶ An analogy is made of two pairs of words. The words in each pair are related in the same way. Complete the following analogies. Accept reasonable responses.

1. *Tidal* is to the *tides* as *seasonal* is to _____.

2. *Source* is to *origin* as *instrument* is to _____.

3. The *Nile* is to *Africa* as the _____ is to *North America*.

4. A *delta* is to the *end* as _____ is to the *beginning*.

5. A *river* is to *natural* as _____ is to *man-made*.

6. *Saltwater* is to _____ as *freshwater* is to *lakes*.

7. _____ is to *liquid* as *glacier* is to *solid*.

8. *Dry* is to *rain forest* as _____ is to *desert*.

▶ Now try this. For each analogy, choose at least one word from the box. Complete a pair of related words. Then write another pair that is related in the same way.

| forest | ocean | coastline | windswept |
| climate | foliage | landscape | wind |

9. _____ is to _____

as _____ is to _____.

10. _____ is to _____

as _____ is to _____.

11. _____ is to _____

as _____ is to _____.

Vocabulary Power

Name _____

CLASSIFY/CATEGORIZE

In each group below, the words or phrases are all related to a word from the box. Write the word that labels the category. Add an animal or a descriptive phrase that fits each category.

| amphibian | arachnid | vertebrate | mammal |
| crustacean | reptilian | amphibious | invertebrate |

1. A tiger
   B ape
   C wolf

   Category: _____mammal_____

   Add: _____(any mammal)_____

2. A crow
   B fox
   C trout

   Category: _____vertebrate_____

   Add: _____(any vertebrate)_____

3. A scorpion
   B daddy longlegs
   C tick

   Category: _____arachnid_____

   Add: __Possible response: spider__

4. A tortoise
   B lizard
   C snake

   Category: _____reptilian_____

   Add: __Possible response: alligator__

5. A toad
   B salamander
   C newt

   Category: _____amphibian_____

   Add: __Possible response: frog__

6. A usually aquatic
   B outer shell
   C may have claws

   Category: _____crustacean_____

   Add: __Possible responses: crab, lobster, barnacle__

7. A jellyfish
   B earthworm
   C octopus

   Category: _____invertebrate_____

   Add: __(any insect, worm, or mollusk)__

8. Write an adjective that describes something that lives or works both on land and in the water

   _____amphibious_____

88 Unit 5 • Chapter 30

Vocabulary Power

Name _____

WORD FAMILIES

Words may be related by a root or base word, or by word parts. For each group below, determine what word part the words have in common. Then add another word that belongs to the same family. The first has been done for you. *Possible responses are given.*

1. **A** amphibious
   B amphitheatre
   C amphipod

   Family: _____*amphi-*_____

   Add: _____amphibian_____

2. **A** amphibian
   B veteran
   C German

   Family: _____*-an*_____

   Add: _____*librarian*_____

3. **A** vertebrate
   B unfortunately
   C tolerated

   Family: _____*-ate*_____

   Add: _____*invertebrate*_____

4. **A** mammal
   B medical
   C capital

   Family: _____*-al*_____

   Add: _____*rural*_____

5. **A** invertebrate
   B incorrect
   C inactive

   Family: _____*in-*_____

   Add: _____*invalid*_____

6. **A** waterfall
   B water buffalo
   C watering can

   Family: _____*water*_____

   Add: _____*water cooler*_____

7. **A** semiannual
   B semisweet
   C semifinal

   Family: _____*semi-*_____

   Add: _____*semicircle*_____

8. **A** January
   B primary
   C stationary

   Family: _____*-ary*_____

   Add: _____*elementary*_____

Vocabulary Power

Name _____

COMPARE AND CONTRAST

Think about the similarities and differences between the words in each pair. Write a phrase or sentence to compare them, or tell how they are alike. Then write a phrase or sentence to contrast them, or tell how they are different. Possible responses are given.

1. **crustacean, invertebrate**

    Compare: _____Crustaceans are invertebrates; they have no spine._____

    Contrast: _____Not all invertebrates are crustaceans._____

2. **arachnid, insect**

    Compare: _____Both are generally small and have more than four legs._____

    Contrast: _____Insects have only six legs; arachnids have eight._____

3. **fish, amphibian**

    Compare: _____Both live in water._____

    Contrast: _____Amphibians can also live on land._____

4. **salamander, lizard**

    Compare: _____similar in shape_____

    Contrast: _____The salamander is an amphibian; the lizard is a reptile._____

5. **whale, elephant**

    Compare: _____both mammals; both very large_____

    Contrast: _____The whale lives in the ocean; the elephant, on land._____

6. **brown bat, owl**

    Compare: _____both fly, are nocturnal_____

    Contrast: _____The bat is a mammal, the owl is a bird; the bat nests upside down._____

Name _____

RHYMING WORDS

Turn the sentences and phrases below into rhymes by filling in each blank with a word from the Word Box.

| relaxation | repose | recreation | pleasure |
| pastime | leisure | diversion | amusement |

1. **Example:** Take a rest from sneezing.

   _____Repose_____ your nose.

2. There is no way to tell how much I enjoy soccer!

   You cannot measure my _____pleasure_____!

3. An activity that is only done during July and August.

   a summertime _____pastime_____

4. A place set aside for those who need to unwind from a hard day.

   a _____relaxation_____ station

5. Someone who likes to work all the time and does not want to be

   disturbed has an aversion to _____diversion_____.

6. The ballpark closed down and the team had to find somewhere else to play.

   This was a case of _____recreation_____ relocation.

7. I felt trapped inside all day by the heavy rains. My puppy thought it was a lot of fun having me at home all day.

   My imprisonment was my puppy's _____amusement_____.

8. These piano lessons have taken all my free time from me.

   I would call that a seizure of my _____leisure_____!

Vocabulary Power   Unit 6 • Chapter 31   91

Name _____

SYNONYMS

▶ The words in the box are all related to recreation. Sort them into the diagram below according to their meaning.

| amusement | pastime | pleasure | recreation |
| diversion | leisure | repose | relaxation |

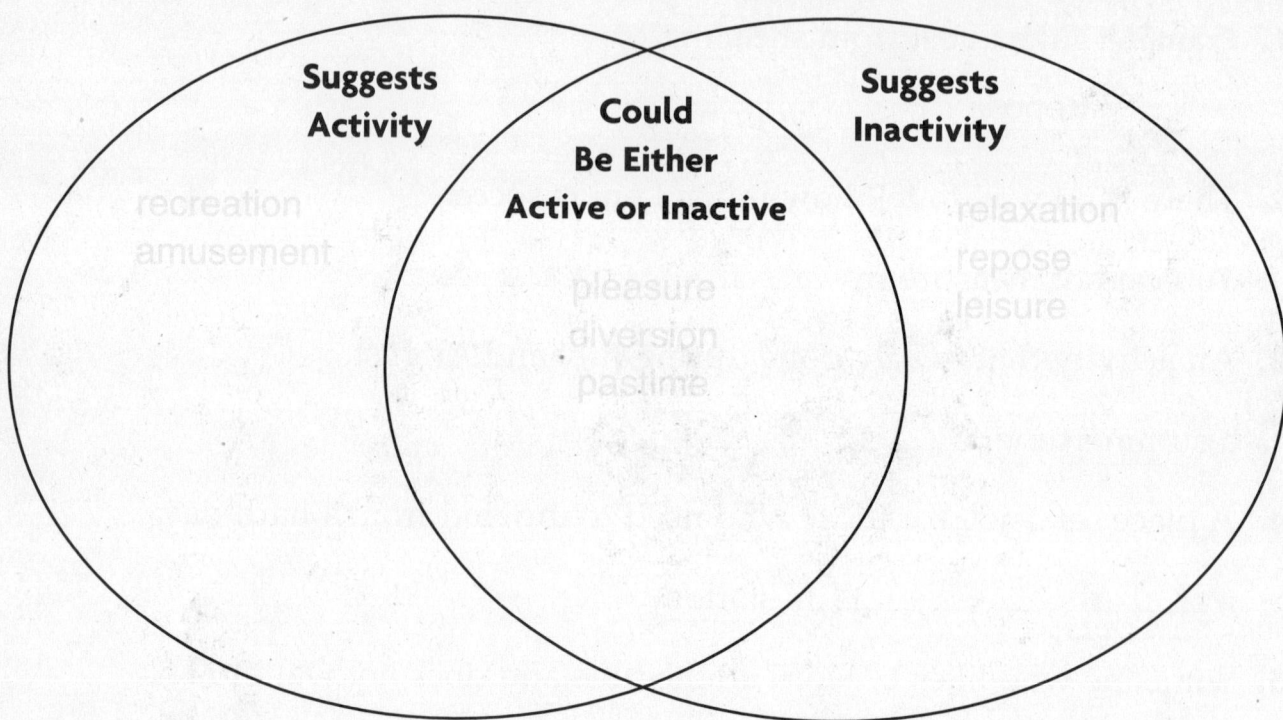

Suggests Activity: recreation, amusement

Could Be Either Active or Inactive: pleasure, diversion, pastime

Suggests Inactivity: relaxation, repose, leisure

▶ Now make a list of pastimes, or kinds of recreation, that are active and a list of pastimes that are not active. Accept reasonable responses.

Active Pastimes

Possible responses: baseball, biking, soccer, swimming, basketball, running, flying a kite

Inactive Pastimes

Possible responses: reading, board games, stamp collecting, listening to music, correspondence

Name _____

CONNOTATION/DENOTATION

▶ Think about the meanings of the underlined words. Answer the questions with complete sentences. Responses will vary. Accept reasonable responses.

1. Would you prefer to do something for <u>amusement</u> or <u>relaxation</u>? Why?

   _____

   _____

2. Would you play soccer for <u>pleasure</u> or for <u>repose</u>? Explain.

   _____

   _____

3. Which is something you might make plans for, <u>recreation</u> or <u>leisure</u>? Explain why you think as you do.

   _____

   _____

4. Which do you take more seriously, a <u>hobby</u> or a <u>pastime</u>? Explain why you think as you do.

   _____

   _____

▶ The following pairs have similar meanings. Circle the word that has a more positive connotation. Explain your choice.

5. (energetic)   aggressive

   Accept reasonable explanations.

6. irritable   (excitable)

   _____

7. uncivilized   (rugged)

   _____

8. (forgetful)   negligent

   _____

Vocabulary Power

Name _____

COMPARE AND CONTRAST

▶ In the left column are names that tell about a person's level of experience or skill. Along the top are several features that may or may not apply to each label. Fill in each block as follows:

        + yes   – no   +/– maybe

Next, add two features of your own that apply to a few of the labels. Fill in each block as before.

	Paid	In training	Proficient	Experienced	Related to Sports	Related to Hobbies		
amateur	–	+/–	+/–	+/–	+	+		
beginner	+/–	+	–	–	+	+		
dabbler	–	+/–	–	–	+	+		
fledgling	+/–	+	–	–	+	+		
novice	+/–	+	–	–	+	+		
professional	+	–	+/–	+/–	+	–		
rookie	+	+	–	–	+	–		
trainee	+	+	–	–	+/–			
expert	+/–	–	+	+	+	+		
veteran	+/–	–	+	+	+	+		

▶ Work with a partner to discuss and compare your completed charts.

Name _____

EUPHEMISMS

A **euphemism** is a word used instead of another word that may have an unpleasant connotation. Using a euphemism makes something sound nicer than it may really be.

▶ In each pair below, the second sentence restates the first, using a euphemism. Complete each by replacing the underlined word(s) with a word from the box below. The first has been done for you.

beginner	antique	fledgling	novice

1. You say: That skateboard is <u>old and run-down</u>.

   I reply: No, it's an _____antique_____.

2. You say: You're just a _____fledgling_____ photographer.

   I reply: No. I'm an <u>amateur</u>, but I do have experience.

3. You say: You <u>don't know what you're doing</u>.

   I reply: I'm a _____beginner_____.

4. You say: A _____novice_____ like Jim isn't good enough for our team.

   I reply: He's a <u>rookie</u>. I think you should give him a chance.

▶ Now try this. One sentence is given to you. Write a second sentence using a euphemism for the underlined word or phrase. You may replace it with a word or a phrase. The first has been done for you.

5. You say: I'm going to get drenched in that <u>downpour</u>!

   I reply: Oh, that's just a little drizzle.

6. You say: The paint on that sign has <u>practically disappeared</u>. I can't even read it.

   I reply: Possible response: The paint does seem a little dull.

Vocabulary Power   Unit 6 • Chapter 32   95

Name _____

ANTONYMS

Choose antonym pairs from the box that match the pairs of definitions given.

| professional | rookie | dabbler | trainer |
| amateur | expert | trainee | veteran |

1. paid ___professional___

   unpaid ___amateur___

2. enjoys something but doesn't take it seriously ___dabbler___
   studies carefully and has a lot of knowledge about something
   ___expert___

3. has spent many years in this job ___veteran___

   this is the first year in this job ___rookie___

4. is learning how to do a job ___trainee___

   is teaching someone how to do a job ___trainer___

COLLOQUIALISMS

A **colloquialism** is a way of saying something informally. For example, a *buck* is a colloquialism for a *dollar*.

Match the colloquialism to the underlined word in each sentence.

| pro | R & R | rookie |

1. The police captain assigned an experienced officer to work with the <u>recruit</u>. ___rookie___

2. Teresa hopes to be a <u>professional</u> golfer one day. ___pro___

3. Ed went to the beach for some <u>rest and recreation</u>. ___R & R___

CLASSIFY/CATEGORIZE

The words in the left column are all adjectives with similar meanings. Check the appropriate boxes to show how each word may be used. Then add some descriptive words of your own and check the boxes as before.

	Describes Language	Describes an Image	Describes a Person
vivid	✓	✓	
colorful	✓	✓	✓
descriptive	✓		
emphatic	✓		
radiant		✓	✓
vibrant		✓	
picturesque	✓	✓	
vivacious			✓

Additional words will vary. Accept reasonable responses.

Vocabulary Power

Name _____

WORDS IN CONTEXT

Think about the meaning of the underlined word. Then respond to each question or complete each sentence.

1. A picturesque description would give readers or listeners a(n) _____
   Possible response: picture/image in their minds of the thing being described.

2. The painting showed a radiant sunset behind the mountains. Describe what might make it seem *radiant*. Possible response: There might be rays of light shining through openings in the clouds.

3. Which of the following words might describe an emphatic speech?

   assertive ✓   soothing ___   demanding ✓

   timid ___   uncertain ___   powerful ✓

4. Write five colorful words to describe a parade.
   Possible responses: brilliant, shining, golden, scarlet, glittery

5. Write five descriptive words to tell about a tree.
   Possible responses: sturdy, shady, leafless, gnarled, ancient

6. Name three or more animals, plants, or things that have vibrant colors.
   Possible responses: a parrot, a kaleidoscope, a cardinal, a neon sign

7. Would you like to have a vivacious friend? Explain your reasons.
   Possible response: Yes; a vivacious person would be friendly and full of life and would be fun to be around.

Name _____

WORD LINES

Arrange each group of words on a word line. Explain how you decided to arrange them. The first one is done for you. Possible responses are given.

1. fast, quick, rapid, speedy, swift

   quick, fast, speedy, swift, rapid

   Each word expresses something a degree faster than the one before.

2. vivid, lifelike, descriptive, picturesque

   descriptive, picturesque, lifelike, vivid

   Each word describes a more lifelike quality than the one before.

3. brilliant, bright, radiant, colorful, vibrant

   bright, colorful, radiant, vibrant, brilliant

   Each word describes something a shade brighter than the one before.

4. blast, boom, bang, roar, thunder

   bang, boom, blast, thunder, roar

   Each word indicates a louder noise than the one before.

5. bit, crumb, dot, drop, grain

   grain, dot, drop, crumb, bit

   Each word indicates something larger than the one before.

6. glad, happy, joyful, merry, cheerful

   glad, cheerful, happy, merry, joyful

   Each word is happier than the one before.

Vocabulary Power   Unit 6 • Chapter 33   99

Name _____

ANALOGIES

An analogy is made of two pairs of words. The words in each pair are related in the same way. Think about the relationships in the following pairs of words. Then fill in the blank to complete the analogy.

Possible responses are given.

1. A *competition* is to a *competitor* as a *sculpture* is to a _____sculptor_____.

2. A *rival* is to an *opponent* as a *victor* is to a _____winner_____.

3. A *tournament* is to *athletic* as an *exhibition* is to _____artistic_____.

4. A *conflict* is to a *disagreement* as a _____contest_____ is to a *competition*.

5. A *contender* is to a *title* as an *heir* is to a _____throne/crown_____.

6. A *finish line* is to a *race* as an _____index_____ is to a *book*.

7. *Lanes* are to a *swimming pool* as _____margins/lines_____ are to a *notebook*.

8. An *entry form* is to a *contest* as an _____application_____ is to a *job*.

9. A *trophy* is to a *prize* as a _____(any vegetable)_____ is to a *vegetable*.

10. *Champion* is to *championship* as *sportsman* is to _____sportsmanship_____.

RHYMING WORDS

Think of another way to say the first sentence in each pair. Choose a word that rhymes with the underlined word.

1. Due to rain, the match ended before a winner was decided.

   The _____meet_____ was <u>incomplete</u>.

2. I'm pretty sure there's going to be an argument.

   I <u>predict</u> a _____conflict_____.

3. I waited for the girl I was competing against to get here.

   I waited for the <u>arrival</u> of my _____rival_____.

100 Unit 6 • Chapter 34   Vocabulary Power

Name _____

WORD FAMILIES

Words can be related by a root or base word, or by word parts. In each group of words below, determine how the words are related. Then circle the letter of the word that is not related to the other three. The first has been done for you.

1. A competition
   (B) compromise
   C compete
   D competitor

   Family: _____Base word *compete*_____

2. A contend
   B contender
   C contention
   (D) competition

   Family: _____Base word *contend*_____

3. A opponent
   B opposition
   C oppose
   (D) oppossum

   Family: _____Base word *oppose*_____

4. A rival
   (B) rivet
   C rivalry
   D rivalrous

   Family: _____Base word *rival*_____

5. A victory
   B victor
   C victorious
   (D) victim

   Family: _____Base word *victor*_____

6. **(A)** torn
   B tourist
   C tournament
   D tourmaline

   Family: _____letter pattern *tour*_____

7. A meet
   (B) neatly
   C fleet
   D greeting

   Family: _____Letter pattern *eet*_____

8. A conflict
   B confusion
   C contract
   (D) counter

   Family: _____Word part *con-*_____

Vocabulary Power   Unit 6 • Chapter 34   101

Name _____

CLASSIFY/CATEGORIZE

Circle the letter of the word that doesn't belong in each list. Then name the category in the space provided. Possible responses are given.

1. **A** contest
   B meet
   C tournament
   (D) players

   Name for category: _____types of competitions_____

2. **F** opponent
   G contestant
   (H) referee
   J contender

   Name for category: _____people taking part in a competition_____

3. **A** tennis
   B badminton
   C volleyball
   (D) cycling

   Name for category: _____games played with a net_____

4. **F** infield
   (G) goal line
   H home plate
   J pitcher's mound

   Name for category: _____parts of a baseball diamond_____

5. **A** batting helmet
   B catcher's mask
   C chest guard
   (D) shoulder pads

   Name for category: _____protective gear worn by baseball players_____

Name _____

ANALOGIES

▶ Each pair of words in an analogy is related in the same way. Complete the following analogies. Responses may vary. Accept reasonable responses.

1. *Strength* is to *weakness* as *rapidly* is to _____.

2. *Revitalize* is to *vigor* as *organize* is to _____.

3. *Vitamin* is to *health* as _____ is to *mathematics*.

4. *Vital* is to *essential* as *running shoes* are to _____.

5. *Deficient* is to *supplement* as *thirsty* is to _____.

6. *Lungs* are to *breathe* as *feet* are to _____.

7. *Vitality* is to *weariness* as *confidence* is to _____.

8. *Red* is to *tomato* as *green* is to _____.

9. *Pears* are to _____ as *broccoli* is to *spinach*.

10. *Wheat* is to _____ as *milk* is to *dairy*.

▶ Now try this. Complete each analogy by writing two pairs of words that are related in the same way. You may choose a word or words from the box, or write words of your own. The first one is started for you.

| round | orange | soccer | exercise |
| color | book | pastime | reading |

11. Orange _____ is to color _____ as _____ is to _____.

12. _____ is to _____ as _____ is to _____.

13. _____ is to _____ as _____ is to _____.

14. _____ is to _____ as _____ is to _____.

Vocabulary Power

Name _____

LATIN ROOTS

The words listed below come from the Latin word *vita*, which means "life." Read each definition. Then choose one of the words to complete each sentence below. Use the part of speech identified in the definitions as a clue for which word to choose.

> **revitalize** *verb* to give new life or energy to
>
> **vitamin** *noun* a substance found in food and needed for the body's health and growth
>
> **vital** *adjective* 1. necessary to or supporting life 2. very important or necessary
>
> **vitality** *noun* 1. vigor, energy 2. the capacity to live, grow, and develop
>
> **vitalize** *verb* 1. to endow or provide with life 2. to invigorate or animate
>
> **vitals** *noun* those bodily organs whose functioning is essential to life

1. We get ____vitamin____ C from eating certain foods.

2. Healthy lungs are ____vital____ to life.

3. Three balanced meals a day help ensure a person's ____vitality____.

4. Warm clothing is ____vital____ for a ski vacation.

5. The phrase "full of vim, vigor, and ____vitality____" is often used to describe a person who is full of energy.

6. A person's ____vitals____ include the brain, the heart, and the lungs.

7. A hearty breakfast will ____vitalize____ you for the day.

8. When you have been sitting still for a long time, exercise is a great way to ____revitalize____ the body.

Name _____

CONTEXT CLUES

Read the sentences below and circle the letter of the best definition of the underlined word. Use context to figure out the meaning of the word.

1. Vitamins are <u>essential</u> to good health. They give you energy and keep you from getting sick.
   - **(A)** of great importance
   - **B** possibly helpful
   - **C** harmful
   - **D** of little importance

2. A medical test can show if you are vitamin-<u>deficient</u>. If you are, you may need to eat a lot of foods that are rich in vitamins.
   - **A** capable of doing a good job
   - **B** not easily achieved
   - **(C)** lacking the necessary amount
   - **D** put off until a later date

3. In addition to eating a healthful, balanced diet, some people also take a vitamin <u>supplement</u>. This gives them an extra dose of important vitamins.
   - **A** a kind of geometric angle
   - **(B)** something in addition to the main source
   - **C** something good you say about another person
   - **D** soft and bendable

4. Increased energy, or <u>vigor</u>, is the result of maintaining a balanced diet and of regular exercise.
   - **A** a feeling of weakness
   - **(B)** bodily strength
   - **C** electric current
   - **D** a type of exercise

5. After hiking for many hours, we swam in the cool lake and rested in the shade. We soon felt <u>revitalized</u> and ready to head back to camp.
   - **A** of importance to good health
   - **B** ready to go to sleep
   - **C** drained of energy; extremely tired
   - **(D)** renewed in energy or liveliness

Vocabulary Power

Unit 6 • Chapter 35   105

Name _____

WORD FAMILIES

Words can be related by a root or base word. They may also be related by word parts. Read each group below and determine how the words are related. Cross out the one word that does not belong to that family, and then add another word that fits. The first has been done for you.

Possible responses are given.

1. A persistent
   B persisting
   (C) persevere
   D persistence

   Family: base word *persist*

   Add: persist

2. A prevail
   B present
   C prepare
   (D) person

   Family: prefix *pre-*

   Add: prevent

3. A utterance
   (B) prevail
   C endurance
   D perseverance

   Family: suffix *-ance*

   Add: disturbance, entrance

4. A strive
   B live
   C driver
   (D) diva

   Family: letter pattern *ive*

   Add: dive, give

5. (A) afloat
   B perpetuate
   C elongate
   D grate

   Family: word part *-ate*

   Add: date, state

6. (A) evening
   B endure
   C encircle
   D encyclopedia

   Family: prefix *en-*

   Add: entertain, enclose

7. A continue
   B discontinue
   (C) contain
   D continual

   Family: base word *continue*

   Add: continuation

8. A unwrap
   B unpack
   (C) under
   D uncooked

   Family: prefix *un-*

   Add: unwind

106 Unit 6 • Chapter 36   Vocabulary Power

Name _____

COMPARE AND CONTRAST

Complete the following sentences to describe how the two items in italic type are alike or how they are different. Responses will vary. Accept reasonable responses.

1. A *tortoise* is like a *turtle* except that _____

2. *Perseverance* is like *persistence* except that _____

3. A *desert* is like a *beach* because _____

4. *To quit* is like *to surrender* except that _____

5. *To persist* is like *to strive* because _____

6. A *race* is like a *test* but _____

7. *Tiring* is like *exhausting* except that _____

8. *To endure* is like *to continue* but _____

9. A *folktale* is like a *legend* because _____

Vocabulary Power

Name _____

CONTEXT CLUES

Read each sentence, paying attention to the meaning of the underlined word. Write a definition for the word as it is used in the sentence.

Possible responses are given.

1. I strive to do my best at dance class, but I'm still not very good at it.

   Strive means try very hard .

2. Hard work will prevail when all else fails.

   Prevail means succeed .

3. The cyclist could not endure the heat of the sun and rested until it became cooler.

   Endure means put up with .

4. We will perpetuate our traffic problems by continuing to buy more cars without expanding the roadways.

   Perpetuate means cause something to last or go on forever .

5. Although learning a new language was difficult, I persevered, and now I can speak Spanish.

   Persevered means did not give up because of difficulty .

6. John's persistence paid off. He found the baseball that his friends had thought was lost.

   Persistence means unwillingness to give up when others do .

7. The setting of the story was a desert in the southwestern United States.

   Setting means the time and/or place in which a story takes place .

8. Similar to a hare, a jackrabbit is a desert-dwelling animal with oversized ears that help it stay cool.

   A *jackrabbit* is an animal that looks like a hare with very large ears .

Glossary

a·bra·sion [ə·brā′zhən] *n.* The process of wearing or rubbing something away: **Daily** *abrasion* **from shoes wore down the wooden floor.**

a·cry·lic [ə·kril′ik] *adj.* Made of or having to do with a special kind of plastic: **I prefer to use** *acrylic* **paint for outdoor scenes.**

al·pine [al′pīn] *adj.* Of, like, or located in mountains: **The** *alpine* **cottage is tucked between two mountains.**

am·a·teur [am′ə·chŏor] *n.* A person who performs an activity for enjoyment rather than for money: **The hero in the play at our community theater is an** *amateur.*

am·bi·ance [am′bē·əns] *n.* A surrounding atmosphere: **The artist's studio had a cheerful** *ambiance.*

am·phib·i·an [am·fib′ē·ən] *n.* An animal that can live both on land and in water: **The salamander, like every** *amphibian,* **is cold-blooded.**

am·phib·i·ous [am·fib′ē·əs] *adj.* Living or adapted to living on land or in water: **The swamp was full of** *amphibious* **plants.**

a·muse·ment [ə·myōoz′mənt] *n.* The condition of being entertained; enjoyment: **The children shared hours of** *amusement* **during their visit to the zoo.**

a·nat·o·my [ə·nat′ə·mē] *n.* The scientific study of the structure of plants or animals: **Brianna will study** *anatomy* **next year.**

an·ces·tor [an′ses·tər] *n.* A person from whom one is descended: **My** *ancestor* **sailed from France to Louisiana in the 1850s.**

ap·prox·i·mate·ly [ə·prok′sə·mit·lē] *adv.* Close to; about: **Our city got** *approximately* **5 inches of rain last month.**

a·quat·ic [ə·kwät′ik] *adj.* Living or growing in or on water: **Water lilies are an** *aquatic* **plant.**

a·que·duct [ak′wə·dukt′] *n.* An artificial channel for carrying water: **We learned about an ancient** *aqueduct* **in Rome.**

a·rach·nid [ə·rak′nid] *n.* Any of a class of animals with four pairs of legs but no antennae or wings: **My dad doesn't like spiders or any other** *arachnid.*

ar·bor·e·tum [är′bə·rē′təm] *n.* A place where trees and shrubs are grown for study: **The** *arboretum* **has unusual plants from Asia.**

arc·tic [är(k)′tik] *adj.* Of or having to do with the region of the North Pole: **Researchers must wear heavy coats to protect themselves against the** *arctic* **wind.**

ar·id [ar′id] *adj.* Without enough rainfall to grow things; dry: **The Sahara is one of the most** *arid* **regions on earth.**

ar·range·ment [ə·rānj′mənt] *n.* The way in which something is ordered: **The art teacher fussed over the** *arrangement* **of the new paintings.**

arts [ärts] *n., pl.* Fields of study that include literature, philosophy, and languages, but not the sciences: **Study of the** *arts* **is essential to a balanced education.**

as·ter [as′tər] *n.* A plant with flowers like daisies: **The** *aster* **growing in my garden has purple petals.**

as·ter·isk [as′tər·isk] *n.* A mark shaped like a star (*) used to show a note is provided: **The** *asterisk* **in the text reminded me to look at the footnote.**

as·ter·oid [as′tə·roid] *n.* Any of thousands of tiny planets orbiting the sun between Mars and Jupiter: **Ceres, the first known** *asteroid,* **was discovered in 1801.**

a add	e end	o odd	ōō pool	oi oil	th this		*a* in *above*
ā ace	ē equal	ō open	u up	ou pout	zh vision		*e* in *sicken*
â care	i it	ô order	û burn	ng ring		ə =	*i* in *possible*
ä palm	ī ice	ŏŏ took	yōō fuse	th thin			*o* in *melon*
							u in *circus*

as•tral [as′trəl] *adj.* Of or relating to the stars: **The observatory made nightly *astral* observations.**

as•tro•dome [as′trə•dōm′] *n.* A transparent dome on the top of an aircraft: **The navigator checked the position of the stars through the *astrodome*.**

as•tro•naut [as′trə•nôt′] *n.* A person who is trained to travel in or fly a spacecraft: **The *astronaut* will attempt a space walk.**

as•tro•nau•tics [as′trə•nô′tiks] *n.* The science of flight in space: **Specialists in *astronautics* will design parts for the space shuttle.**

as•tron•o•mer [ə•stron′ə•mər] *n.* A person who studies stars, planets, and other space objects: **Johannes Kepler, a German *astronomer*, discovered that the planets follow oval-shaped orbits.**

at•mos•phere [at′məs•fir] *n.* The air surrounding the earth: **The *atmosphere* is made of mostly nitrogen and oxygen.**

auc•tion•eer [ôk′shən•ir′] *n.* A person who conducts an auction (a public sale): **The *auctioneer* kept the sale moving.**

au•di•to•ry [ô′də•tôr′ē] *adj.* Of or having to do with hearing: **The *auditory* nerves connect the inner ear to the brain.**

au•to•bi•og•ra•phy [ô′tə•bī•og′rə•fē] *n.* The story of a person's life written by that person: **The famous dancer wrote her *autobiography*.**

au•to•graph [ô′tə•graf′] *n.* A person's own signature: **I waited at the arena to get my favorite star's *autograph*.**

bare•ly [bâr′lē] *adv.* Only just; scarcely: **We have *barely* enough snow for a snowman.**

be•gin•ner [bi•gin′ər] *n.* A person who has little experience or is doing something for the first time: **Every *beginner* at the piano recital was nervous.**

bi•og•ra•phy [bī•og′rə•fē] *n.* The story of a person's life and experiences: **Juanita read a *biography* of Thomas Jefferson before writing her report.**

blos•som [blos′əm] *v.* To develop or grow; flourish: **The young dancers will *blossom* under the famous ballerina's teaching.**

bo•tan•i•cal [bə•tan′i•kəl] *adj.* Having to do with plants or with botany: **The *botanical* show attracts thousands of gardeners each spring.**

bot•an•ist [bot′ən•ist] *n.* A scientist who studies plants and plant life: **The *botanist* closely examined the needles of the cactus.**

bot•a•ny [bot′ə•nē] *n.* The study of plants: **Madison has decided to study *botany* instead of zoology.**

boul•e•vard [bŏŏl′ə•värd′] *n.* A broad city street or main road, often lined with trees: **The parade ran the entire length of the *boulevard*.**

bris•tle [bris′(ə)l] *n.* Coarse, stiff hair, often used for brushes: **I cleaned the *bristles* of the brush after I finished painting.**

budg•et [buj′it] *n.* A plan for spending money over a period of time: **I will save money if I stay within my *budget*.**

busi•ness [biz′nis] *n.* A commercial or industrial enterprise: **The only *business* on Main Street is a clothing store.**

ca•nal [kə•nal′] *n.* A waterway constructed across land: **A *canal* is often an important shipping route.**

can•vas [kan′vəs] *n.* A cloth surface specially prepared for a painter to use: **The artist dabbed paint onto the *canvas*.**

car·ni·val [kär′nə·vəl] *n.* An amusement show, typically with rides and shows: **This year's *carnival* will have a Ferris wheel.**

car·ou·sel [kar′ə·sel′] *n.* A merry-go-round: **The children enjoyed riding the *carousel*.**

chance [chans] *n.* A possibility or opportunity: **Give him another *chance* to succeed.**

cho·re·o·graph [kôr′ē·ə·graf′] *v.* To make up combinations of steps to create a dance: **I want to *choreograph* my own performance.**

cho·re·og·ra·pher [kôr′ē·og′rə·fər] *n.* A person who creates dance movements: **The *choreographer* explained what the dancers were to do.**

cir·cum·stance [sûr′kəm·stans′] *n.* A condition: **Ice on the roads is a *circumstance* that may cause traffic accidents.**

civ·ic [siv′ik] *adj.* Of or having to do with a city: **The mayor asked the citizens to do their *civic* duty and vote.**

civ·i·li·za·tion [siv′ə·lə·zā′shən] *n.* The society and culture of a particular people, place, or period: **Archaeological remains in South America provide important information about the Inca *civilization*.**

cli·mate [klī′mit] *n.* The kind of weather a place has over a period of time: **Tropical islands often have a pleasant *climate*.**

coast·al [kōs′təl] *adj.* Of, on, or near the coast: **Charleston, South Carolina, is a *coastal* city.**

coast·line [kōst′līn′] *n.* The outline or border of a coast: **The *coastline* of New England is beautiful on sunny days.**

col·or·ful [kul′ər·fəl] *adj.* Full of bright colors: **The leaves are *colorful* in autumn.**

com·pe·ti·tion [kom·pə·tish′ən] *n.* A contest: **Diane is an excellent artist, and she usually wins the annual watercolor *competition* at the museum.**

com·pose [kəm·pōz′] *v.* To create: **Mr. Gonzalez will *compose* a letter to the school board.**

com·po·si·tion [kom′pə·zish′ən] *n.* The parts that make up something: **Our science teacher explained the *composition* of the air we breathe.**

con·duct [kən·dukt′] *v.* To lead a musical group: **Mr. Saunders will *conduct* the orchestra on Sunday.**

con·duc·tor [kən·duk′tər] *n.* A person who leads or guides, usually for an orchestra or chorus: **The orchestra members watched the *conductor* for the cue to begin playing.**

con·flict [kon′flikt] *n.* A struggle, fight, or battle: **Several nations sent troops to help end the *conflict*.**

con·ten·der [kən·ten′dər] *n.* A person who participates in a competition: **The senator is a *contender* for the presidential nomination.**

con·tin·u·ous [kən·tin′yōō·əs] *adj.* Going on without any pause or interruption: **Our homes and schools need a *continuous* supply of electricity.**

cred·it [kred′it] *n.* Any deposit or sum of money against which a person may draw: **I received store *credit* for the sweater that I returned.**

a add	e end	o odd	ōō pool	oi oil	th this	ə =	a in *above*
ā ace	ē equal	ō open	u up	ou pout	zh vision		e in *sicken*
â care	i it	ô order	û burn	ng ring			i in *possible*
ä palm	ī ice	ŏŏ took	yōō fuse	th thin			o in *melon*
							u in *circus*

crus•ta•cean [krus•tā′shən] *n.* An animal, such as a lobster or crab, with a tough outer shell and a segmented body that lives in water: **The largest *crustacean* is the giant spider crab.**

cui•sine [kwi•zēn′] *n.* A style or type of cooking: **I like Mexican *cuisine*, but my sister likes Japanese *cuisine*.**

cul•ture [kul′chər] *n.* The ideas and way of life of a group of people at a particular time. Culture includes language, customs, music, art, food, and games. **In North American *culture*, people shake hands when they meet.**

cur•ren•cy [kûr′ən•sē] *n.* Money in general use that is available for exchange: **I will exchange my American dollars for Mexican *currency* before I leave.**

dab•bler [dab′lər] *n.* Someone who does something, but not very seriously: **Nathan is a serious painter, but I'm only a *dabbler* in art.**

debt [det] *n.* An amount that a person owes to another: **Letisha owes Kim a *debt* of five dollars.**

ded•i•ca•tion [ded′ə•kā′shən] *n.* The act of setting apart for or devoting to a special purpose: **The mayor and governor attended the *dedication* of the park.**

de•fi•cient [di•fish′ənt] *adj.* Not complete: **His understanding of fractions is *deficient*.**

del•ta [del′tə] *n.* The flat plain at a river's mouth made of soil that the river has carried downstream: **The Nile River creates a vast *delta* in northern Egypt.**

de•mol•ish [di•mol′ish] *v.* To tear down completely; destroy: **The bulldozer will *demolish* the abandoned house.**

de•scrip•tive [di•skrip′tiv] *adj.* Telling what a person or thing is like: **The magazine is full of *descriptive* articles about towns in Texas.**

de•stroy [di•stroi′] *v.* To ruin completely: **One tornado can *destroy* a neighborhood.**

dev•as•tate [dev′ə•stāt] *v.* To leave in ruins; destroy: **The approaching hurricane is likely to *devastate* the island.**

di•a•ry [dī′(ə•)rē] *n.* A book or journal in which one writes about personal events, experiences, and thoughts: **I like to write in my *diary* before I go to sleep at night.**

di•ur•nal [di•ûrn′əl] *adj.* Of or happening during the day: ***Diurnal* animals are awake during the day and asleep at night.**

di•ver•sion [di•vûr′zhən] *n.* An amusement, game, or pastime done for relaxation or distraction: **The crossword puzzle was a pleasant *diversion* on the long car trip.**

down•town [doun′toun′] *adv.* In the main business district of a town or city: **When you are *downtown*, you can take the subway or the bus.**

drench [drench] *v.* To wet thoroughly; soak: **If we don't find an umbrella, the rain will *drench* us.**

ea•sel [ē′zəl] *n.* A frame on legs used to hold canvas or paper for painting, a chart, or other items: **Our teacher placed the map on an *easel*.**

e•con•o•my [i•kä′nə•mē] *n.* The system of earning and managing money or resources in a family, business, or community of any size: **The national *economy* is strong.**

em•phat•ic [em•fat′ik] *adj.* Done or spoken with forceful speech: **Our mother was *emphatic* about our cleaning the playroom.**

em•ploy•ment [im•ploi′mənt] *n.* A job or

occupation: **She found *employment* at the bank.**

en•dure [in•d(y)o͞or′] *v.* To put up with; bear; tolerate: **Athletes must sometimes *endure* pain during an event.**

en•gi•neer [en′jə•nir′] *n.* A person who is trained in the skill of putting scientific knowledge to practical use, as in the construction of roads, bridges, and machinery: **The city hired an *engineer* to plan the new highway.**

en•ter•tain [en•tər•tān′] *v.* To hold the attention of and give enjoyment to: **Our dog, Buddy, can *entertain* the neighborhood children for hours.**

e•ro•sion [i•rō′zhən] *n.* The gradual wearing away of soil or rock by water or wind: **The powerful waves from the storm caused severe *erosion* of the beach.**

es•sen•tial [i•sen′shəl] *adj.* Extremely important or necessary; vital: **It is *essential* that you unplug the iron when you finish using it.**

eth•ni•ci•ty [eth•nis′ət•ē] *n.* The characteristics of a particular group, such as race, country of origin, religion, or culture: **The *ethnicity* of the neighborhood is mixed.**

ex•act•ly [ig•zakt′lē] *adv.* Precisely; just so: **The train ride lasted *exactly* fifteen minutes.**

ex•tra-sen•si•tive [ek′strə-sen′sə•tiv] *adj.* Especially capable of feeling or reacting quickly or easily: **My uncle is *extra-sensitive* about his nickname.**

ex•traor•di•nary [ik•strôr′də•ner′ē *or* ek′strə•ôr′də•ner′ē] *adj.* Remarkable; unusual; surprising: **The fireworks on Independence Day were *extraordinary*.**

fa•ble [fā′bəl] *n.* A short story that teaches a lesson, often using animals as characters: **My sister's favorite *fable* is "The Crow and the Pitcher."**

fic•tion [fik′shən] *n.* A form of literature whose characters and events are entirely or partly imaginary: **The author's newest story is a work of *fiction*.**

fledg•ling [flej′ling] *n.* A young, inexperienced person; beginner: **Unlike the older violinists, I am only a *fledgling*.**

flo•ra [flôr′ə] *n.* All the plants of a particular place or period of time: **The *flora* of Florida includes many kinds of palm trees.**

flour•ish [flûr′ish] *v.* To grow vigorously; thrive: **Many different plants can *flourish* on tropical islands.**

flow•er [flou′ər] *n.* The part of a plant or tree that encloses the seeds; blossom: **The *flower* on this plant has bright yellow petals.**

fo•li•age [fō′lē•ij *or* fō′lij] *n.* The leaves on a tree or other plant: **The *foliage* on this plant comes out after the flowers do.**

folk•lore [fōk′lôr′] *n.* The beliefs, stories, and customs preserved among a people: **Paul Bunyan is a popular character in American *folklore*.**

folk•tale [fōk′tāl′] *n.* A traditional story handed down by word of mouth: **The story of Johnny Appleseed is an American *folktale*.**

form [fôrm] *n.* A mold, frame, or model that gives shape to something: **The toy company made a *form* to produce a new doll.**

a add	e end	o odd	o͞o pool	oi oil	th this		a in *above*
ā ace	ē equal	ō open	u up	ou pout	zh vision	ə =	e in *sicken*
â care	i it	ô order	û burn	ng ring			i in *possible*
ä palm	ī ice	o͝o took	yo͞o fuse	th thin			o in *melon*
							u in *circus*

113

frame [frām] *n.* A basic inner structure that gives support and shape to the thing built around it: **The skyscraper's *frame* is made of steel.**

frame·work [frām'wûrk'] *n.* The basic inner structure around which a thing is built: **Our cabin has a wooden *framework*.**

G

ge·ne·al·o·gy [jē'nē·al'ə·jē *or* jē'nē·ol'ə·jē] *n.* A record of the ancestors and descent of a person or family: **Aunt Lucy is the expert on our family's *genealogy*.**

ge·og·ra·pher [jē·og'rə·fər] *n.* A person who studies the features of the earth's surface: **The small island was mapped by a *geographer*.**

ge·ol·o·gist [jē·ol'ə·jist] *n.* A scientist who studies the history and structure of the earth: **A *geologist* visited our class and explained the history of several rocks.**

gild·ed [gil'dəd] *v.* Covered or coated with a thin layer of gold: **He *gilded* the front of the picture frame.**

gla·cier [glā'shər] *n.* A large mass of ice that moves very slowly: **An immense *glacier* covers much of Antarctica.**

grav·el [grav'əl] *n.* A mixture of small pebbles and pieces of rock: **It is difficult to ride our bikes on *gravel*.**

grav·i·ty [grav'ə·tē] *n.* The pull of stars, planets, and moons on objects near them: **Astronauts are weightless in space because they are beyond earth's *gravity*.**

green·house [grēn'hous'] *n.* A heated building, usually made of glass, that is used for growing plants: **We can grow flowers in the *greenhouse* during the winter.**

H

hab·i·tat [hab'ə·tat] *n.* The place where an animal or plant naturally lives or grows: **The *habitat* of goldfish is fresh water.**

hap·pen·stance [hap'ən·stans'] *n.* A chance occurrence: **It was just *happenstance* that we met in the park.**

he·red·i·ty [hə·red'ə·tē] *n.* The passing on of characteristics from parents to children by means of genes: **My hair is blond and my eyes are brown because of *heredity*.**

her·i·tage [her'ə·tij] *n.* Traditions or customs handed down from one generation to the next: **Texas has a *heritage* of pride and independence.**

his·to·ry [his'tə·rē] *n.* Past events, or a record of them, often concerning a particular nation, people, or activity: **Our class is studying the *history* of the United States.**

hy·drate [hī'drāt] *v.* To cause to take up water: **Drink plenty of fluids to *hydrate* yourself before, during, and after exercise.**

I

im·pres·sion [im·presh'ən] *n.* Any mark made by pressing: **My shoes made an *impression* in the thick carpet.**

in·ac·cu·rate·ly [in·ak'yər·it·lē] *adv.* Incorrectly: **The news team *inaccurately* reported the time and place of the robbery.**

in·her·i·tance [in·her'ə·təns] *n.* Something obtained from someone upon his or her death, by will or law: **Mrs. Lopez received an antique watch as an *inheritance*.**

in·let [in'let' *or* in'lət] *n.* A narrow strip of water leading inland from a larger body of water: **The boats are kept in the *inlet*, where the water is calmer.**

in·ter·view [in'tər·vyoo] *n.* A meeting between two or more people for the purpose of obtaining information: **A reporter will have an *interview* with the**

invertebrate — metropolitan

mayor to find out about the new city library.

in•ver•te•brate [in•vûr′tə•brit *or* in•vûr′tə•brāt′] *n.* An animal without a backbone: **An ant is an *invertebrate*.**

ir•ri•gate [ir′ə•gāt′] *v.* To bring water to land by using pipes, ditches, or canals: **The farmers *irrigate* their crops by pumping water from the nearby lake.**

jew•el•er [jōō′əl•ər *or* jōō′lər] *n.* A person who sells, repairs, or makes jewelry: **The *jeweler* showed wedding rings to the couple.**

jour•nal [jûr′nəl] *n.* A daily account of events or thoughts: **I wrote in my *journal* every day I was at camp.**

land•scape [land′skāp′] *n.* A stretch of natural scenery on land as seen from a single point: **From the top of the mountain, you can see the *landscape* of the whole park.**

lan•guage [lang′gwij] *n.* The words that a certain nation or group uses in speaking and writing: **English is an official *language* of South Africa.**

leg•a•cy [leg′ə•sē] *n.* Money or property that has been left to one by a will: **His aunt left him a generous *legacy* when she died.**

lei•sure [lē′zhər *or* lezh′ər] *n.* Time free from work, study, or other duties: **During summer vacation, Tyrone has the *leisure* to skate with his friends.**

lit•er•a•ture [lit′ər•ə•chŏŏr] *n.* Written works that show imagination and artistic skill: **The author has won many awards for her contributions to children's *literature*.**

live•li•hood [līv′lē•hŏŏd′] *n.* The means by which one supports one's life: **How do you earn your *livelihood*?**

mag•ma [mag′mə] *n.* The hot, partly liquid mass of rock within the earth: **When *magma* moves to the surface of the earth, it becomes lava.**

mam•mal [mam′əl] *n.* Any vertebrate animal the females of which produce milk to feed their offspring: **The blue whale, the largest living animal, is a *mammal*.**

ma•rine [mə•rēn′] *adj.* Having to do with, formed by, or found in the sea: **Some *marine* animals live deep below the surface of the ocean.**

mar•i•ner [mar′ə•nər] *n.* A sailor: **The *mariner* raised the sails of his small boat.**

mar•i•time [mar′ə•tīm′] *adj.* Of or having to do with the sea: **Captains of ships must be familiar with *maritime* laws.**

me•an•der [mē•an′dər] *v.* To wind or turn, as a path or river: **The streams *meander* through the forest.**

meet [mēt] *n.* An assembly or gathering, as for a sports event: **Tomorrow I have a track *meet*.**

me•lo•di•ous [mə•lō′dē•əs] *adj.* Pleasant to hear; musical: **The singer has a *melodious* voice.**

mem•oir [mem′wär] *n.* The story of a person's own life and experiences: **Presidents sometimes write a *memoir* about their time in office.**

met•ro•pol•i•tan [met′rə•pol′ə•tən] *adj.* Of or having to do with a large city: **The**

a add	e end	o odd	ōō pool	oi oil	th this		a in *above*
ā ace	ē equal	ō open	u up	ou pout	zh vision	ə =	e in *sicken*
â care	i it	ô order	û burn	ng ring			i in *possible*
ä palm	ī ice	ŏŏ took	yōō fuse	th thin			o in *melon*
							u in *circus*

metropolitan area has many old neighborhoods.

mois·ten [mois′ən] *v.* To make slightly wet or damp: **Please *moisten* the stamp and place it on the envelope.**

mold [mōld] *n.* A hollow form that gives a particular shape to something soft or liquid: **The toy figures are made by pouring hot plastic into a *mold*.**

mon·u·ment [mon′yə·ment] *n.* Something, such as a building, statue, or arch, built in memory of a person or event: **The Jefferson Memorial is a *monument* in Washington, D.C.**

moun·tain·eer [moun′tən·ir′] *n.* A mountain climber: **Aaron, who is a *mountaineer*, has climbed Mount Rainier twice.**

mu·ni·ci·pal [myōō·nis′ə·pəl] *adj.* Of or having to do with a town or city or its local government: **There are three *municipal* parking garages downtown.**

mu·si·cal [myōō′zi·kəl] *adj.* Of, having to do with, or related to music: **Do you play a *musical* instrument?**

myth [mith] *n.* A traditional story, often offering an explanation of something in nature or of past events: **I read a *myth* about why the snow leopard is white.**

nar·ra·tive [nar′ə·tiv] *n.* An account, story, or tale: **The detectives asked the suspects for a *narrative* of their activities on the day of the robbery.**

nau·ti·cal [nô′ti·kəl] *adj.* Of or having to do with ships, sailors, or the sea: **The admiral looked closely at a *nautical* map as he plotted the fleet's next move.**

na·val [nā′vəl] *adj.* Of, for, done by, or having to do with the navy: **An ensign is the lowest ranking *naval* officer.**

near·ly [nir′lē] *adv.* Almost; practically; close to: **It is *nearly* time for lunch.**

noc·tur·nal [nok·tûr′nəl] *adj.* Of or happening at night: **The campers were not afraid of the *nocturnal* sounds.**

non·fic·tion [non′fik′shən] *adj.* Writing that is true and does not contain imaginary events or characters: **The magazine contains *nonfiction* articles as well as creative stories.**

nov·ice [nov′is] *n.* A beginner or inexperienced person: **Eric is still a *novice* at basketball, but he is learning quickly.**

o·a·sis [ō·ā′sis] *n.* An area in the desert made fertile by a water supply: **In contrast to the barren desert, the *oasis* had palm trees and green bushes.**

ob·lit·er·ate [ə·blit′ə·rāt′] *v.* To destroy completely: **Elise watched the fire *obliterate* an old shed.**

oc·ca·sion [ə·kā′zhən] *n.* An important event: **All of my friends were with me for the happy *occasion*.**

oc·cu·pa·tion [ok′yə·pā′shən] *n.* The work by which a person earns a living: **Her *occupation* is newspaper reporter.**

oc·cur·rence [ə·kûr′əns] *n.* The act or fact of something happening or taking place: **The unexpected *occurrence* of the disease worried the doctors.**

o·ce·an·ic [ō′shē·an′ik] *adj.* Of, living in, or produced by the ocean: **The ship will be the scientists' *oceanic* home for a month.**

oc·u·lar [ok′yə·lər] *adj.* Of, having to do with, or like the eye: **After giving me an *ocular* exam, the optometrist fitted me for eyeglasses.**

ol·fac·to·ry [ol·fak′tər·ē] *adj.* Of or having to do with the sense of smell: **People with**

a poor sense of taste may have a limited *olfactory* sense as well.

op•pon•ent [ə•pō′nənt] *n.* A person who takes the opposite side in a fight, game, or contest: **She faced her *opponent* on the other soccer team.**

op•por•tu•ni•ty [op′ər•tyōō′nə•tē] *n.* A right or convenient time, occasion, or circumstance: **I had the *opportunity* to visit a national park this summer.**

or•ches•trate [ôr′kəs•trāt′] *v.* To arrange music for an orchestra: **A professional composer will *orchestrate* our winter musical.**

or•der [ôr′dər] *n.* A special or particular arrangement of things one after the other: **Put these words in alphabetical *order*.**

or•gan•i•za•tion [ôr′gən•ə•zā′shən] *n.* The act or condition of being in good order: **The *organization* of my desk helps me find things easily.**

or•i•gin [ôr′ə•jin] *n.* The beginning of the existence of anything: **The *origin* of that story is unknown.**

or•nate [ôr•nāt′] *adj.* Fancy or showy: **The house had an *ornate* mirror hanging in the hall.**

ox•y•gen [ok′sə•jin] *n.* A colorless, tasteless, odorless gas: **One-fifth of the earth's atmosphere is *oxygen*.**

o•zone [ō′zōn′] *adj.* An unstable form of oxygen that has a sharp odor: ***Ozone* is found naturally in earth's upper atmosphere.**

pal•ette [pal′it] *n.* A board used by an artist for mixing and holding paints: **The artist's *palette* held a rainbow of colorful oil paints.**

pas•time [pas′tīm′] *n.* Something that makes time pass pleasantly, as a sport or hobby: **Stephen's favorite *pastime* is reading.**

ped•es•tal [ped′is•təl] *n.* The base that supports a column, a statue, or a vase: **I accidentally bumped the *pedestal*, and the vase toppled to the floor.**

pe•des•tri•an [pə•dəs′trē•ən] *n.* A person who travels on foot: **A *pedestrian* could easily fall into that hole in the sidewalk.**

per•cep•tion [pər•sep′shən] *n.* The ability to become aware of things by means of senses: **My visual *perception* was not very good in the dark room.**

per•form [pər•fôrm′] *v.* To give an exhibition of artistic skill before an audience: **The choir will *perform* for the whole school.**

per•pet•u•ate [pər•pech′ōō•āt′] *v.* To cause to last a very long time: **He left money in his will to *perpetuate* the good deeds he had done for the community.**

per•se•ver•ance [pûr′sə•vir′əns] *n.* The continuing attempt to do something in spite of difficulties: **With much *perseverance*, she was able to finish the race.**

per•se•vere [pûr′sə•vîr′] *v.* To keep trying in spite of difficulties: **My science teacher encouraged me to *persevere* in my study of space.**

per•sist [pər•sist′] *v.* To continue firmly in spite of opposition, warning, or difficulty: **Jen and Karen *persist* in their batting practice, hoping to hit home runs.**

per•sis•tence [pər•sis′təns] *n.* The act of continuing firmly in spite of opposition, warning, or difficulty: **Her *persistence* and**

a	add	e	end	o	odd	ōō	pool	oi	oil	th	this		a in *above*
ā	ace	ē	equal	ō	open	u	up	ou	pout	zh	vision		e in *sicken*
â	care	i	it	ô	order	û	burn	ng	ring			ə =	i in *possible*
ä	palm	ī	ice	ōō	took	yōō	fuse	th	thin				o in *melon*
													u in *circus*

positive attitude helped her achieve her goal.

pe·tro·le·um [pə·trō′lē·əm] *n.* A dark, thick, oily liquid found in the earth and used to make fuels: **Gasoline is made from *petroleum*.**

pho·to·graph [fō′tə·graf′] *n.* A picture made with a camera: **My grandmother has a *photograph* of her mother as a young girl.**

pho·tog·ra·pher [fə·tog′rə·fər] *n.* A person who takes pictures with a camera: **The *photographer* took pictures of everyone at the wedding.**

pic·tur·esque [pik′chə·resk′] *adj.* Having the kind of beauty suitable for a painted picture: **The village, nestled in the valley beside an orchard, is quite *picturesque*.**

pi·o·neer [pī′ə·nir′] *n.* Someone who leads the way, as in developing a new field: **He was a *pioneer* in computer engineering.**

plaque [plak] *n.* A metal, wood, or stone plate with writing on it attached to a wall or object to identify a person, place, or event: **Tourists were reading the *plaque* on a statue.**

plea·sure [plezh′ər] *n.* A feeling of enjoyment, delight, or satisfaction: **My cats give me great *pleasure*.**

po·di·a·trist [pə·dī′ə·trəst] *n.* A doctor who treats injuries and other problems related to feet: **I visited a *podiatrist* when I had an ingrown toenail.**

po·e·try [pō′ə·trē] *n.* The art of writing poems: ***Poetry* has been popular since ancient times.**

po·si·tion [pə·zish′ən] *n.* A job; employment: **She has an excellent *position* as principal of a school.**

pre·cise·ly [pri·sīs′lē] *adv.* Accurately; exactly: **Can you tell us *precisely* when the train will arrive?**

pre·vail [pri·vāl′] *v.* To gain control; be victorious: **We hope our soccer team will *prevail* in the championship match.**

pro·ba·bil·i·ty [prob′ə·bil′ə·tē] *n.* The likelihood of something happening: **The *probability* that it will snow today is low.**

pro·fes·sion [prə·fesh′ən] *n.* A field of work that requires thinking rather than physical labor: **There are many different careers to choose from in the medical *profession*.**

pro·fes·sion·al [prə·fesh′ən·əl] *adj.* Working for money in a field often entered by amateurs: **She is a *professional* athlete.**

pro·gress [prə·gres′] *v.* To advance toward a goal; develop; improve: **Our teachers expect us to *progress* quickly in our study of history.**

pro·gres·sion [prə·gresh′ən] *n.* A series or sequence, as of events: **A *progression* of events led to our move to Dallas.**

pros·per [pros′pər] *v.* To be successful; thrive: **Our town will *prosper* when the new factories open.**

pur·suit [pər·s(y)o͞ot′] *n.* An activity that is regularly done or followed, as a profession, hobby, or sport: **Scuba diving is a thrilling and fascinating *pursuit*.**

R

ra·di·ant [rā′dē·ənt] *adj.* Very bright and shining; brilliant: **The *radiant* sun reflected off the snow.**

rec·re·a·tion [rek′rē·ā′shən] *n.* An enjoyable activity or other form of amusement, relaxation, or play: **My sister and I play tennis for *recreation*.**

re·fur·bish [rē·fûr′bish] *v.* To brighten or freshen up; redecorate or renovate: **My parents will *refurbish* the apartment before we move in.**

re·lax·a·tion [rē'lak·sā'shən] *n.* The act of resting from work or exercise: **For *relaxation*, he read a book beside the pool.**

ren·o·vate [ren'ə·vāt'] *v.* To make something look like new; freshen; repair: **The school will *renovate* our media center during the summer.**

re·pose [ri·pōz'] *n.* Rest or sleep: **The artist painted a woman in contented *repose*.**

rep·til·i·an [rep·til'ē·ən] *adj.* Of, having to do with, or characteristic of a reptile: **We found a nest of *reptilian* eggs beside the pond.**

re·sour·ces [ri·sor'sez *or* rē·sôr'səz] *n., pl.* A supply of something that can be used or drawn on: **They had the cash *resources* to buy a new car.**

re·store [ri·stôr'] *v.* To bring back to a former or original condition: **Polishing will help *restore* the wooden desk.**

re·vi·ta·lize [rē·vīt'əl·īz'] *v.* To give new life or energy to something: **Another win will *revitalize* the discouraged team.**

re·vive [ri·vīv'] *v.* To bring or come back to life or consciousness: **The doctors can *revive* him once he reaches the hospital.**

ri·val [rī'vəl] *n.* A person who tries to equal or outdo another; competitor: **We will be playing our *rival* in the play-offs.**

rook·ie [rook'ē] *n.* A beginner or novice, as in a professional sport: **Although Pamela is just a *rookie*, she scored three times in her first game.**

ro·ta·ting [rō'tā·ting] *v.* Turning around, as if on an axis: **The earth is *rotating* constantly.**

rough·ly [ruf'lē] *adv.* About; approximately: ***Roughly* 100 students voted in the election today.**

scaf·fold [skaf'əld *or* skaf'ōld] *n.* A temporary structure put up to support workers and materials; any raised framework: **The *scaffold* is ten stories high.**

sculpt [skulpt] *v.* To form a figure or representation of one from a solid material, as by carving or shaping: **Tomorrow we will *sculpt* a person's head.**

sed·i·ment [sed'ə·mənt] *n.* Matter that settles to the bottom of a liquid: **The swift river carried *sediment* into the lake.**

seis·mo·graph [sīz'mə·graf'] *n.* An instrument that records the strength and duration of earthquakes: **A *seismograph* in Arizona detected an earthquake in California.**

sen·a·tor [sen'ə·tər] *n.* A member of a governing body known as the senate: **The *senator* voted against the bill.**

se·quel [sē'kwəl] *n.* A work that continues a story begun in a previous work: **The director's second movie is a *sequel* to his first one.**

se·quence [sē'kwəns] *n.* The order of arrangement in which one thing comes after another: **Our teacher asked us to discuss the *sequence* of events in the story.**

ser·en·di·pi·ty [ser'ən·dip'ə·tē] *n.* The act of finding good things by accident: **It was *serendipity* that I spotted the ten-dollar bill on the ground.**

skel·e·ton [skel'ə·tən] *n.* The internal framework of bones that supports the body of a vertebrate animal: **We studied the**

human *skeleton* in science class.

sky·scra·per [skī′skrā′pər] *n.* A very high building: **The tallest *skyscraper* in Chicago is the Sears Tower.**

sluice [slo͞os] *n.* An artificial channel used for transporting water: **The farmer lowered the gate so that no water could pass through the *sluice*.**

smog [smog] *n.* A blend of smoke and fog: ***Smog* hangs over the city in the summertime.**

so·ci·e·ty [sə·sī′ə·tē] *n.* A group of persons living in a particular place or at a particular time and having many things in common: **Canadian *society* is like that of many European countries.**

source [sôrs] *n.* The beginning of a stream or river: **The *source* of the Nile River is Lake Victoria.**

spe·cial·i·za·tion [spesh′ə·lə·zā′shən] *n.* A topic or subject about which someone knows a lot: **The doctor's *specialization* is heart surgery.**

spend·ing [spend′ing] *n.* The act of paying money for goods or services: **If you are going to save money, you need to decrease your *spending*.**

strive [strīv] *v.* To make a strong effort: **Please *strive* to learn the vocabulary words.**

struc·ture [struk′chər] *n.* A building of any kind: **There is only one *structure* on the farm.**

sub·ject [sub′jikt] *n.* The person, thing, or idea that one deals with, as in writing or painting: **The old cabin was the *subject* of the mural.**

sub·ma·rine [sub′mə·rēn′] *n.* A ship that operates on or under the surface of the sea: **The *submarine* surfaced less than a mile offshore.**

sub·se·quent [sub′sə·kwənt] *adj.* Following in time, place, or order: ***Subsequent* events proved us right.**

sub·ter·ra·ne·an [sub′tə·rā′nē·ən] *adj.* Located or happening under the earth: **The *subterranean* tunnels were converted into an extensive subway system.**

sub·way [sub′wā′] *n.* An electric railroad that is mainly underground: **We can take the *subway* to the museum.**

suc·ceed [sək·sēd′] *v.* To accomplish what is planned or intended: **She will *succeed* in learning all of the multiplication tables before the test.**

sup·ple·ment [sup′lə·mənt] *n.* Something that adds to or completes: **The magazine added a *supplement* to cover the recent events.**

sur·round·ings [sə·roun′dingz] *n., pl.* The things or conditions around a person or place; environment: **Our school has pleasant *surroundings*.**

sur·vive [sər·vīv′] *v.* To remain alive or in existence; outlast: **This kind of tree can *survive* for hundreds of years.**

tem·per·ate [tem′pər·it] *adj.* Moderate in temperature: **Many parts of the United States enjoy a *temperate* climate.**

thrive [thrīv] *v.* To grow vigorously: **Fish *thrive* in the waters off the coast of Maine.**

ti·dal [tīd′(ə)l] *adj.* Of, having to do with, or caused by the tides: **After the tide went out, we splashed in the *tidal* pools.**

tour·na·ment [to͝or′nə·mənt *or* tûr′nə·mənt] *n.* A series of matches in a sport or game involving many players or teams: **A chess *tournament* is scheduled for tomorrow after school.**

train•ee [trā′nē′] *n.* A person who is being taught how to do something, as in a job: **My sister is a *trainee* at the bank.**

trans•at•lan•tic [trans′ət•lan′tik] *adj.* Across or crossing the Atlantic Ocean: **Amelia Earhart was the first woman to make a *transatlantic* flight alone.**

trans•con•ti•nen•tal [trans′kän′tə•nen′təl] *adj.* Stretching from one side of continent, or major land mass, to the other: **The first *transcontinental* railroad was completed in the United States in the nineteenth century.**

trans•late [trans•lāt′] *v.* To change something written or spoken into another language: **I can *translate* this story into Spanish.**

trans•lu•cent [trans•lōō′sənt] *adj.* Clear enough to allow light, but not images, to pass through: **The frosted glass in the bathroom window is *translucent*.**

trans•moun•tain [trans•moun′tən] *adj.* Crossing or extending through or over a mountain: **Driving through the *transmountain* tunnel was quicker than driving around the mountain.**

trans•o•ce•an•ic [trans′ō•shē•an′ik] *adj.* Crossing over or under the ocean: ***Transoceanic* telephone cables lie at the bottom of the Pacific and Atlantic oceans.**

trans•par•ent [trans•pâr′ənt] *adj.* Allowing light to pass through so images can be clearly seen; clear: **Windshields are *transparent*.**

trans•port [trans•pôrt′] *v.* To carry from one place to another: **The moving trucks will *transport* our furniture to our new house.**

trib•u•tar•y [trib′yə•ter′ē] *n.* A stream flowing into a larger stream or body of water: **The *tributary* from the mountain floods the river during springtime.**

trop•i•cal [trop′i•kəl] *adj.* Of, having to do with, or located in the hot and humid region known as the tropics: ***Tropical* forests contain many plants and animals.**

trough [trôf] *n.* A long, narrow, open container for holding food and water for animals: **The farmer added feed to the *trough*.**

ur•ban [ûr′bən] *adj.* Having to do with a city or city life: **We moved away from the *urban* area to live on a small farm.**

val•ley [val′ē] *n.* The low area between hills and mountains: **The *valley* was full of shadows in the early morning and late afternoon.**

va•por [vā′pər] *n.* Moisture in the form of water droplets floating in the air as mist, fog, or steam: ***Vapor* rose from the lake.**

veg•e•ta•tion [vej′ə•tā′shən] *n.* Plant life: **Many large cities have little *vegetation*.**

ver•te•brate [vûr′tə•brāt′] *n.* Any animal with a backbone: **Dogs are one kind of *vertebrate*.**

vi•brant [vī′brənt] *adj.* Full of energy; vigorous: **Our choir director has a *vibrant* personality.**

vic•tor [vik′tər] *n.* The winner, as in a contest or competition: **The judges are about to give a trophy to the *victor*.**

vig•or [vig′ər] *n.* Active strength or force;

a add	e end	o odd	ōō pool	oi oil	th this		a in *above*
ā ace	ē equal	ō open	u up	ou pout	zh vision	ə =	e in *sicken*
â care	i it	ô order	û burn	ng ring			i in *possible*
ä palm	ī ice	ŏŏ took	yōō fuse	th thin			o in *melon*
							u in *circus*

vitality: **For several weeks after his surgery, Trevor couldn't play baseball with much *vigor*.**

vir·tu·al·ly [vûr′chōō·əl·lē] *adv.* For the most part; practically: **He has read *virtually* every book in the library.**

vi·tal [vīt′(ə)l] *adj.* Having great importance; essential: **The oil fields are of *vital* interest to the nation.**

vi·tal·ity [vī·tal′ə·tē] *n.* Physical or mental energy; liveliness: **Mr. Reynolds is always energetic and full of *vitality*.**

vi·ta·min [vīt′ə·min] *n.* A substance found in food and needed for the body's growth and health: **Many fruits have a lot of *vitamin* C.**

vi·va·ci·ous [vi·vā′shəs *or* vī·vā′shəs] *adj.* Full of life and spirit; lively: **My cousins are *vivacious*, always smiling and laughing.**

viv·id [viv′id] *adj.* Clear and strong: **Her memories of the awards ceremony were *vivid*.**

vo·ca·tion [vō·kā′shən] *n.* A profession, career, or trade: **Is writing his *vocation* or just a hobby?**

vol·can·ic [vol·kan′ik] *adj.* Of, produced by, or thrown up from a volcano: ***Volcanic* ash covered the nearby town.**

vol·un·teer [vol·ən·tir′] *n.* A person who offers to help or to work without pay: **My father is a *volunteer* for the American Red Cross.**

wear [wâr] *v.* To damage or use up: **Too many games of touch football will *wear* the grass in the middle of the yard.**

weath·er·ing [weaŧħ′ər·ing] *n.* The action of natural elements, such as wind and rain, creating changes, especially in rock or soil: **The *weathering* of the cliffs from the storms concerned scientists.**

whirl·i·gig [(h)wûr′lə·gig′] *n.* A merry-go-round: **Many children were lined up to ride the *whirligig*.**

wind·swept [wind′swept] *adj.* Swept by or exposed to the wind: **The *windswept* plains looked vast and empty.**

My Own Word List

My Own Word List